The cost of labor and materials is rising constantly. People are turning to do-it-yourself projects as a means of completing additions and renovations to their houses. If you are a homeowner, a shed significantly increases the value of your property. You will also appreciate the additional storage space that your new shed will provide. This book will enable you to make a new shed a reality if you follow the instructions carefully. Should you ever decide to sell your home, a carefully planned and constructed shed will add considerably to your home's resale value.

BUILD YOUR OWN
Shed
manual

Build Your Own Shed Manual is a unique guide that concentrates on the process of building rather than designing the shed. Certainly all the elements of design and proper plan detailing are considered, but this is foremost a book that graphically demonstrates the latest in shed construction techniques. Each step of the construction process is illustrated in detail. Several design alternatives are presented for your consideration.

You will understand the construction terminology used in this book as you progress. A Shed Glossary is provided on pages 42 and 43 to explain unfamiliar terms. Study the cutaway drawings and captions shown on pages 4 and 5 to help you to envision your shed. On pages 45-77 select from a wide range of predesigned shed plans available for ordering at any time.

Every effort has been made at the time of publication to ensure the accuracy of the information contained herein. However, the reader should check for his or her own assurance and must be responsible for design, selection and use of suppliers, materials and actual construction.

No part of this work covered by the copyright herein may be reproduced or used in any form or by any means - graphic, electronic, or mechanical, including photocopying, recording, taping, or information storage retrieval system - for any purpose other than the purchaser's personal use without the written permission of HDA, Inc. Happy shed building!

Build Your Own Shed Manual is published by HDA, Inc., 944 Anglum Road, St. Louis, MO 63042. All rights reserved. Reproduction in whole or in part without written permission of the publisher is prohibited. Printed in the U.S.A. © 2011. Artist drawings and photos shown in this publication may vary slightly from the actual working drawings. Some photos are shown in mirror reverse. Please refer to the floor plan for accurate layout.

ISBN-10: 0-934039-47-X
ISBN-13: 978-0-934039-47-5

Current Printing (last digit) 5 4 3 2 1

TABLE OF CONTENTS

Build Your Own Shed? 2
Planning Your Shed 2-3
Typical Gable Roof Shed 4
Typical Gambrel Roof Shed 5
Choosing the Right Location 6
Laying Out the Shed Site... 6
Staking Out the Shed 7
Wood Skid and Wood Floor Foundation 8
Concrete Pier and Wood Floor Foundation 9
Concrete Slab Foundation.. 10
Pouring the Concrete Slab 11
Choosing Lumber for Your Shed.. 12-13
Ordering Shed Materials 14
Sample Material List... 14
Nails and Fasteners... 15
Framing with Metal Fasteners... 16-17
Typical Shed Floor Plan.. 18
Typical Shed Wall and Roof Framing Plan............................... 18
Constructing the Basic Wall Frame... 19
Door and Window Framing 20
Diagonal Bracing 21
Raising the Walls 22

Leveling and Corner Details 23
Roof Framing 24-31
Applying Vertical Panel Siding 32
Applying Horizontal Hardboard Siding..................................... 33
Building Paper 33
Overhang Details 34
Corner Trim Details.. 35
Window and Door Details 36
Roof Shingles 37
Installing Electrical Wiring... 38
Finishing the Inside of Your Shed 39
Adding a Ramp to Your Shed.. 40
For Notes and Layout Procedures... 41
Glossary 42-43
Ready to Start Some Serious Planning?.................................. 44
Example of a Typical Project Plan Sheet.................................. 44
Project Plans: Sheds, Playhouses, Cabanas and More ... 45-77
Project Plan Index 78
Before You Order 79
Blueprint Price Schedule.. 79
Shipping and Handling Information 79
Order Form... 80

Build Your Own Shed?

The answer is YES! By doing the planning and all or part of the work yourself, you can have the shed you might not otherwise be able to afford. By supplying the labor and buying materials yourself, construction costs can be cut significantly.

Framing out a shed is not difficult. Standardized materials and construction techniques make it relatively easy if you take time to plan and work carefully.

Planning Your Shed

The key to a successful shed project is planning, planning, and more planning! Once you have begun construction of your shed, it is both costly and time-consuming to correct errors in shed placement, construction, or selection of materials. So the motto of the Do-It-Yourself shed builder must be **PLAN AHEAD!** Whether you choose to draw the plans for your shed following the guidelines in this manual or you decide to purchase a pre-drawn shed plan that is offered on pages 46-77, you must carefully plan all elements of your shed project.

Here is a checklist of design information which you must gather before you begin to design your shed:

❏ **Local Building Requirements -** Visit your local building department and determine how local building codes and zoning ordinances will influence your project. Be prepared to apply for a building permit once you have completed your design.

❏ **Deed Restrictions -** Are there conditions in your property deed that restrict the type and location of your shed? Are you planning to place your shed over property controlled by an easement for right-of-way or utility access?

❏ **Climatic Factors -** Evaluate the microclimate of your intended shed location. Microclimate includes the shading effect of deciduous or evergreen trees and shrubs, the angle of the sun in relation to nearby landscaping during different seasons, soil drainage conditions, and prevailing wind and temperature conditions. Remember that an enclosed shed without temperature regulation needs to be protected from the sun in the summer and exposed to any available in the winter.

❏ **Shed Functions -** What do you want your shed to do? Will your shed serve as a simple shed for gardening and lawn tools or do you plan to use it to store household items? Do you want to supply it with electrical power? What type of storage or shelving units would you like to install in your completed shed? Will your shed include a workshop or hobby area? Careful planning regarding the functions of your shed will save you from costly changes after the project is completed.

❏ **Plan Carefully BEFORE You Begin -** All the techniques and tips you'll need are in this book. Read it carefully before you begin construction. It will help you determine the work you can handle alone and also where expert help might be needed to do the job right. You can also learn many construction basics by studying existing sheds. Ask your neighbors if you can take a few minutes to review their sheds before you begin planning your design.

❏ **Your Budget -** You must determine an estimated dollar amount that you plan to spend on your shed. Do you plan to construct it yourself or will you subcontract with a professional to build the shed after you have purchased materials? Perhaps you want a contractor to complete your shed project in its entirety. It is helpful if you can set upper and lower spending limits so that you can consider options in the materials that you plan for your shed. If you decide to finance your shed project, don't forget to include interest cost in the total cost amount.

❏ **Your Materials Source -** After you have completed your design work and have settled on a bill of materials, you should remember that your local lumber chain or home improvement store is an invaluable resource for the completion of your project. Consult with your local store to check for the materials you require. If special ordering is necessary, determine lead times for the materials. Don't underestimate the importance of a reputable resource like your local home improvement store in providing both quality materials and design knowledge.

Planning Your Shed

The shed site plans on this page are included to exemplify how your shed can contribute valuable storage space to your home. Before you place your shed on your property, study traffic patterns in your backyard and how often you will use the building on a daily basis. Create a site plan of your property and draw arrows to illustrate the basic movements to and from your home. Establish priorities for storage locations and traffic to your proposed shed.

Be aware of problem areas that relate to shed placement. Will you need to build a ramp to move lawn tools in and out of the building? Be certain that you have adequate clearances to move these tools up and down the ramp. If your shed uses clerestory windows for example to supplement or replace electrical lighting, remember that south-facing windows will provide the greatest amount of natural lighting.

Study the site plans shown in Figures 2A to 2D for ideas concerning shed placement. If you create a site plan of your own, remember that it is essential to locate exterior doors and windows on your plan. Try to include all exterior structures and landscaping in your plan. While a scale drawing is not essential, it is not difficult to create a site plan to scale with a ruler and pencil. Grid paper with 1/4" grids is perfect for drawing your preliminary site plan on a 1/4"=1'-0" scale.

These site plans are provided for illustration purposes only. You should sketch your own site plan first and make certain that your proposed shed addition conforms to all applicable building codes before you begin construction. A little time devoted to planning before you begin will save time and money during the construction of your project.

Figure 2B

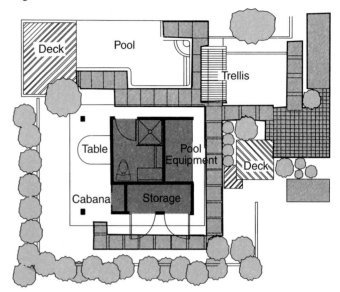

Figure 2C

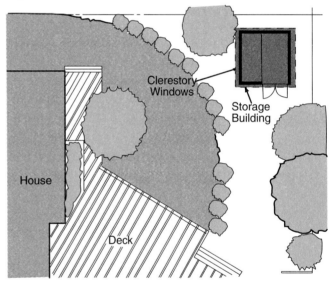

Figure 2D

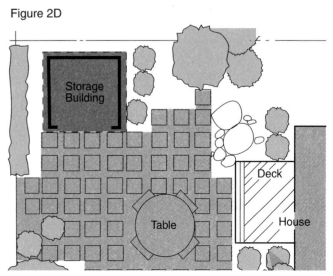

Figure 2A

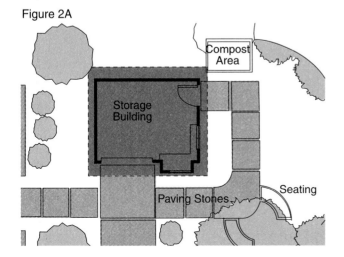

Typical Gable Roof Shed

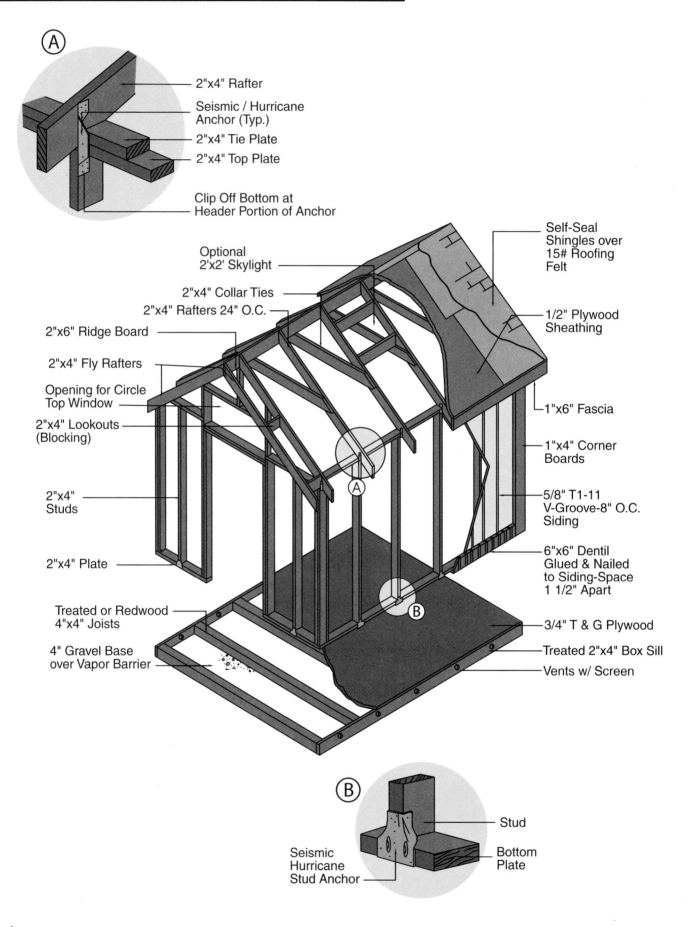

Ⓐ
2"x4" Rafter
Seismic / Hurricane Anchor (Typ.)
2"x4" Tie Plate
2"x4" Top Plate
Clip Off Bottom at Header Portion of Anchor

Optional 2'x2' Skylight
2"x4" Collar Ties
2"x4" Rafters 24" O.C.
2"x6" Ridge Board
2"x4" Fly Rafters
Opening for Circle Top Window
2"x4" Lookouts (Blocking)
2"x4" Studs
2"x4" Plate
Treated or Redwood 4"x4" Joists
4" Gravel Base over Vapor Barrier

Self-Seal Shingles over 15# Roofing Felt
1/2" Plywood Sheathing
1"x6" Fascia
1"x4" Corner Boards
5/8" T1-11 V-Groove-8" O.C. Siding
6"x6" Dentil Glued & Nailed to Siding-Space 1 1/2" Apart
3/4" T & G Plywood
Treated 2"x4" Box Sill
Vents w/ Screen

Ⓑ
Stud
Bottom Plate
Seismic Hurricane Stud Anchor

Typical Gambrel Roof Shed

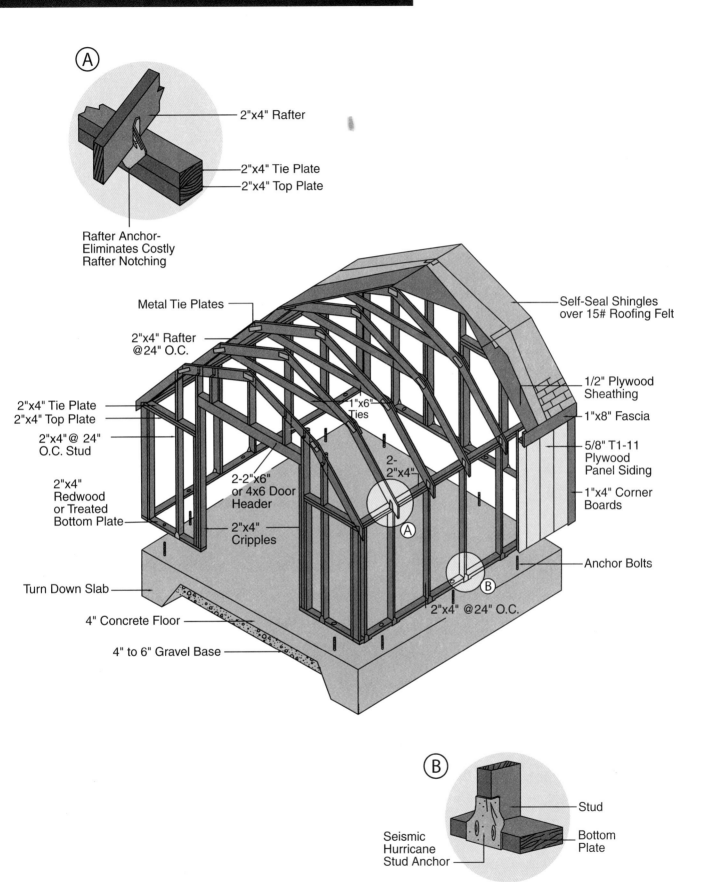

A
- 2"x4" Rafter
- 2"x4" Tie Plate
- 2"x4" Top Plate
- Rafter Anchor- Eliminates Costly Rafter Notching

- Metal Tie Plates
- 2"x4" Rafter @24" O.C.
- 2"x4" Tie Plate
- 2"x4" Top Plate
- 2"x4"@ 24" O.C. Stud
- 2"x4" Redwood or Treated Bottom Plate
- 2-2"x6" or 4x6 Door Header
- 2"x4" Cripples
- 1"x6" Ties
- 2-2"x4"
- Self-Seal Shingles over 15# Roofing Felt
- 1/2" Plywood Sheathing
- 1"x8" Fascia
- 5/8" T1-11 Plywood Panel Siding
- 1"x4" Corner Boards
- Anchor Bolts
- 2"x4" @24" O.C.
- Turn Down Slab
- 4" Concrete Floor
- 4" to 6" Gravel Base

B
- Stud
- Bottom Plate
- Seismic Hurricane Stud Anchor

5

Choosing the Right Location

Before you begin, consult with your local building department and obtain information regarding the placement, height, and square footage of outdoor sheds. For example, your local codes might specify that outbuildings cannot exceed a certain peak to ground height and that a shed must be offset a certain distance from property lines. If you disregard the code restrictions in your municipality, you will create problems for yourself and your neighbors. You might even be forced to remove a structure that violates local code requirements or to pay fines. If your local code requires a permit, submit a site plan and shed construction plans to your local building department and obtain all necessary permits before you begin construction.

Remember that your shed will serve as an important storage addition to your home. With this goal in mind, be certain to select a location that will make shed access convenient but unobtrusive. Sketch a traffic plan that details major access paths in your yard and around your home to help you determine the correct location for your shed.

Consider the building location in relationship to existing and future elements of your landscaping. Don't build a shed next to a tree whose growing roots will displace the shed foundation. Be certain that the placement of your shed in your backyard landscape matches the planned use of the shed. For example, if you want to use the shed in the winter, don't place the shed on the north side of a large evergreen tree which would completely block valuable winter sunlight.

If at all possible, always select a well-drained location for your shed. A spot with poor drainage or soft ground will cause problems later. Water accumulating under the shed creates condensation and can rust the materials you are storing inside.

Laying Out the Shed Site

Accurately locating the four corners of the building will in turn establish the boundaries for the foundation. The site is laid out using batterboards set back from the corners of the planned building in an L-shaped arrangement. Setting the batterboards back from the actual building site allows you to maintain an accurate reference point as you dig footings and construct the foundation (see Figure 6).

Batterboards are made of pointed stakes connected with 4' lengths of 1x4 lumber. Each batterboard should form an accurate right angle when checked with a framing square. Batterboard tops must be level with each other all the way around. Check for levelness with a string level or a mason's line level. Consult the step-by-step instructions on page 7 for help in establishing your site layout.

A variety of shed foundation construction methods are available depending upon your local site and your budget. If you do not want to anchor the shed permanently to one location, consider the wood skids and wood floor foundation detailed on page 8. Alternative foundation options are detailed on pages 9 and 10.

For example, in areas where the ground does not freeze during the winter, pier block foundations offer an inexpensive and sturdy method of anchoring your shed foundation. Pre-cast pier blocks with nailers are readily available at many building supply retailers and provide a relatively simple foundation base for the first time builder.

A more expensive and permanent alternative foundation is the turned-down or monolithic concrete slab. Concrete has the advantage of durability and resistance to moisture damage. If you do select a concrete slab, make sure that your slab will drain properly if moisture is released within your shed. Drainage for concrete slabs is especially important for cabana or greenhouse structures.

Figure 6 - Batterboards

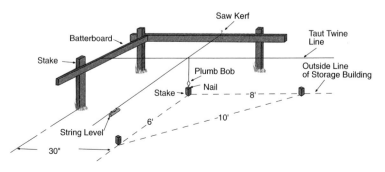

Staking Out the Shed

Figure 7 - Layout Procedure

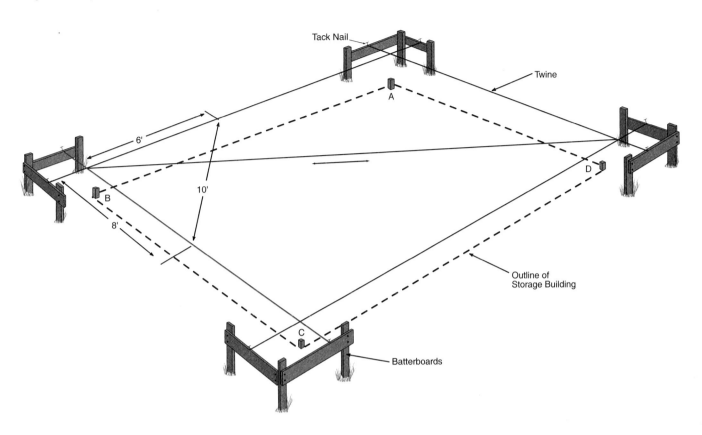

1. Accurately locate one corner of the building and drive stake A at that point (see Figure 7).
2. Measure out along the long side of the building to the next corner. Drive in stake B at this point. Drive a small nail into the stakes and connect with tightly drawn twine.
3. Measure out the approximate positions of corners C and D and drive stakes at these points. Use a framing square to form an approximate right angle at these corners. Run twine from stakes B to C, C to D, and D to A.
4. You will now erect batterboards and adjust stake locations to form a true square or rectangular layout. Erect batterboards so that each corner stake is lined up directly on the diagonal from the opposite corner as illustrated. Use the line level to check that all batterboards are level with each other.
5. Stretch mason's twine between the batterboards so it is aligned directly over stakes A and B. When perfectly aligned make a saw kerf in the batterboards to make a permanent reference point and tack down the twine taut.
6. Stretch twine over stakes B and C. It must form a perfect right angle with twine A-B. Check for a perfect right angle using the 6-8-10 method. Measure 6'-0" out along twine A-B and 8'-0" along twine B-C. Mark these points with pins. The diagonal between these two pins should measure exactly 10'-0". Adjust the position of twine B-C until the diagonal does equal 10'-0" and then notch the batterboard at stake C and fasten off line B-C.
7. Using the 6-8-10 method lay out twine C-D and D-A. At each corner carefully measure from the point where the twine lines cross each other to set building dimensions. Drop a plumb line at this intersecting point and set stakes in exact positions.
8. Check the final layout by measuring the diagonals between foundation stakes. The diagonals must be equal in length if your layout is squared up. If they are not, recheck your measurement and make proper adjustments.

Figure 8 - Skid and Wood Floor Foundation

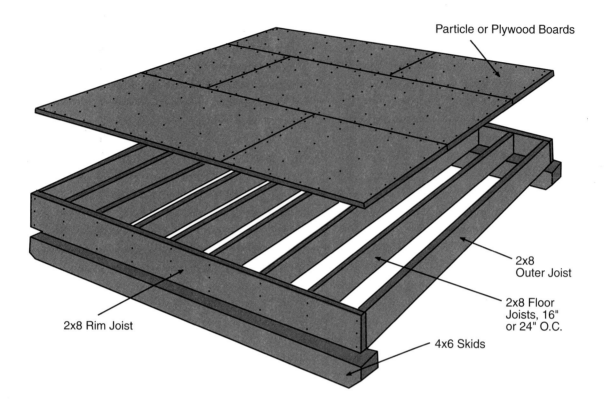

Particle or Plywood Boards

2x8 Outer Joist

2x8 Floor Joists, 16" or 24" O.C.

4x6 Skids

2x8 Rim Joist

1. Site Preparation - Prepare the site by scraping away all grass or weed material covering the shed area. If your soil does not drain well, remove 4"- 6" of earth under the shed area and replace with 4" of pea gravel to increase drainage. Otherwise you can simply dig a drainage trench approximately 12" wide by 6" deep where the 4x6 skids are to be placed. Fill the drainage trench with gravel to ensure good drainage and to minimize the wood to soil contact.

2. Placing the Skids - Skids should be either pressure treated or redwood to prevent decay from ground contact. Position the 4x6 skids and make certain that the skids are level (see Figure 8). Tie the skids together by nailing the outer 2x8 floor joist to the front and rear rim joist. Toenail the outer joist to the skid. If you want to incline the shed floor slightly to ensure drainage, you should raise one end of both skids by an equal amount (1" for every 8' of skid) by placing additional gravel under the skid.

3. Constructing the Floor Frame - Having nailed the rim joist to the skids, you should now check that the floor frame is square. You can use the 6-8-10 method detailed on page 7 to ensure squareness. Complete the floor framing by adding the remaining 2x8 floor joists placed at 16" on center. Connect the floor joists to the rim joists with at least 3-16d coated sinkers at each end. If your budget allows it, use metal joist hangers to add extra strength to your floor joist framing.

4. Adding the Flooring - For extra strength and durability, use 4'x8'x3/4" tongue and groove exterior grade plywood for flooring. For normal use, install 4'x8'x3/4" CDX plywood to construct your floor. Fasten the floor framing to the floor joists using 8d nails 6" on center at the edge of the sheets and 10" on center along the intermediate floor joists. Take care to construct a stable and even floor which will serve as the foundation for your wall sections.

Concrete Pier and Wood Floor Foundation

1. **Site Preparation** - Prepare the site by scraping away all grass or weed material covering the shed area. If your soil does not drain well, remove 4"-6" of earth and replace with 4" of pea gravel to increase drainage.

2. **Locating the Piers** - You will need to use your batterboards (see pages 6-7) to stretch a nylon string along the imaginary outer wall line. Use this string line to stake the pier locations at 4'-0" on center (see Figure 9). The piers will support either a 4x6 beam or a built-up beam made from two 2x6s.

3. **Pre-cast Piers** - If you are using precast concrete piers with an attached wooden nailer, you need to dig a pier footing at least 14" wide and 6" deep. The depth of the footing should be at least 6" below the local frost line. Pour the concrete into the footing hole. Spray the pier with water and then embed the pier at least 3" into the fresh concrete and twist slightly to achieve a solid bond between the concrete and the pier. Make certain that you have enough concrete in the hole so that the top of the nailer block is at least 4"-6" above grade level. Check the alignment of the pier by dropping a plumb bob from the centerline string. Finally, use a level across the block and tap the pier until it is level in all directions and square.

4. **Attach the Beam Support Posts to the Piers** - Cut 4x4 beam support posts to place the floor at a height above grade determined by local codes. If you don't require posts, simply toenail the 4x6 beam into the precast pier nailer blocks with 12d coated sinkers. If you require a certain grade to floor clearance, toenail the posts into the nailer and then use a post cap connector to secure the beam to the post.

5. **Constructing the Floor Framing and Floor** - Follow the methods outlined in steps 3 and 4 on page 8 to construct the floor framing and the wood floor.

Optional Poured In-Place Piers

First be certain you have purchased enough concrete to complete pier installation. Concrete is measured in cubic yards. To calculate the concrete required for a given number of cylindrical piers, use the following formula to find the Total Volume in Cubic Yards:

$$\text{Volume} = \frac{3.14 \times \text{Depth of Pier (feet)} \times \text{Diameter (feet)} \times \text{Diameter (feet)} \times \text{No. Piers}}{108}$$

Example: Concrete required for twelve 10" diameter piers, 30" deep.

$$\text{Volume in cubic yards} = \frac{3.14 \times 2.5 \times .83 \times .83 \times 12}{108} = 0.61$$

*Remember to convert inches to feet (10 inches = .83 feet)
Conversion Factor: 27 Cubic Feet = 1 Cubic Yard

Mix concrete according to manufacturer's instructions in a wheelbarrow or in a "half-bag" mixer. Use clean water for mixing and achieve the proper plastic consistency before you pour the concrete. If you are not using ready-mix concrete, prepare a 1:2:3 mix – one part concrete, two parts river sand, and three parts gravel.

Coat the inside of the forms with oil to prevent sticking and dampen the inside of the hole with water before you pour the concrete.

With your post base anchors at hand, pour the concrete into the forms and tap slightly to settle. For poured in-place piers, wait for the concrete to begin to harden and set the post base anchors into the concrete. Ensure that anchors are square and level. You can drop a plumb bob from your centerline string to be certain that your anchor is centered properly. Adjust post base anchors to the correct height.

Figure 9 - Concrete Pier and Wood Floor Foundation

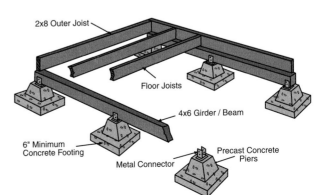

Tapered Pier Form

6" Minimum Concrete Footing

2x8 Outer Joist

Floor Joists

4x6 Girder / Beam

Precast Concrete Piers

Metal Connector

Concrete Slab Foundation

Figure 10 - Concrete Slab Foundation

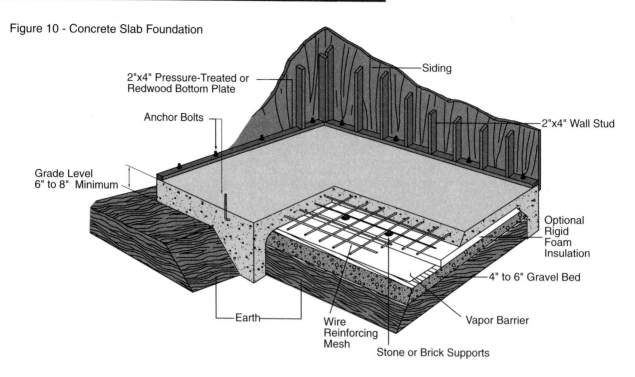

A concrete slab is the most permanent and durable method of constructing a foundation for your shed. However, slab construction requires greater preparation and expense than wood floor construction using skids or concrete piers.

1. **Site Preparation** - Prepare the site by scraping away all grass or weed material covering the shed area. Stake out the area for the slab. Be certain that all corners are square. If you are using a plan for slab construction, remember that all dimensions on the plan are to the outside of concrete. Excavate 4" of soil over shed area and replace with 4" of gravel to ensure proper drainage under slab. Level the gravel fill (see Figure 10).

2. **Digging the Footing** - Dig a trench for the slab footing approximately 8" wide at the bottom and tapering inward to approximately 16" wide at the top. The footing should extend down about 12" or at least 6" below the local frost line.

3. **Building the Forms** - Use 2" scrap lumber to build the forms for the slab. Set the top of the 2" form board to the desired floor height and level. The inside face of form boards must line up exactly with "string lines" set at proper building dimensions. Brace your forms securely since you don't want them to shift or break when concrete is poured.

4. **Preparing to Pour the Concrete** - Place a 6 mil plastic vapor barrier over the gravel bed before you pour. Overlap the plastic sheets by at least 12" and do not puncture the plastic. If you want to insulate your slab from the earth, place 1" rigid foam insulation over the plastic provided that you have allowed for the additional height. Add two levels of 1/2" reinforcing bar (rebar) to the top and bottom of the footing and secure the rebar with tie wire held by nails in the forms. Finally place 6"x6" reinforcing wire mesh over the slab area and support the mesh with small wooden or masonry blocks so that it rests 2" above the vapor barrier.

5. **Estimating the Concrete** - The table to the right will help you estimate the approximate amount of concrete required to create a 4" thick slab with 18" deep footings.

Estimating Concrete

Slab Size	Concrete Required
8' x 12'	2.5 cubic yards
12' x 12'	3.5 cubic yards
12' x 16'	5.0 cubic yards
12' x 20'	6.0 cubic yards

Pouring the Concrete Slab

If necessary, have your local building inspector approve the forms before you pour. If your shed will utilize electrical service or plumbing, place the electrical conduit or plumbing in the proper location before you pour.

Placing

Be prepared for the arrival of the ready-mix truck or you could be charged a wait time fee (see Figure 11A). Have extra helpers, a wheelbarrow, and concrete finishing tools ready. When the truck arrives, pour the area farthest from the truck and fill the footing trench making sure the concrete does not push the forms or rebar out of alignment. For larger areas, break the work into smaller sections by installing temporary screeding guides.

When one section is poured move to the next section while the helpers screed off the first (see Figure 11B). Ask a helper to knock the sides of the forms with a hammer in order to force air pockets out of the concrete. Be sure that all voids are filled with concrete. Pay special attention to the perimeter area of the form boards. Remove the temporary screed guides when you fill in these voids.

Finishing

Once the concrete has lost its initial shine, begin finishing it with a bull float (see Figure 11C). Larger floats have a handle like a broom. If you are using smaller hand floats, use toe and knee boards placed on the concrete so you can kneel on the concrete without leaving much of an impression. Move the float in long sweeping motions.

Anchor bolts should be placed after the concrete has been screeded and bull floated (see Figure 11D). Place the bolts 1-3/4" away from the edge of the slab. Double-check spacing of bolts and alignment.

For a coarser finish, bull floating is all that is required. For a slicker, smoother finish, use a steel trowel to go over the work once bull floating is complete. Use a light touch so you don't gouge the concrete surface. Before the concrete hardens completely, take a trowel and cut between the edge of the concrete and the form.

Curing

Once all finishing is completed, mist down the slab with water, and cover it with a layer of plastic or burlap. Keep the surface moist for four days as the concrete cures.

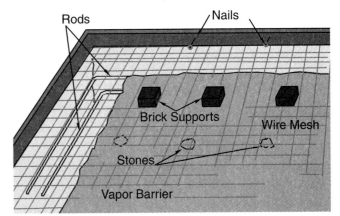

Figure 11A - Steel reinforcing rods and wire mesh are laid into place over gravel and optional plastic vapor barrier.

Figure 11B - Workers level concrete slab with a screed board.

Figure 11C - Smooth concrete surface with a bull float.

Figure 11D - Add anchor bolts.

Choosing Lumber for Your Shed

Figure 13A will give you an idea of some of the defects found in dimensional lumber. Typical defects are checks that result from separation of wood across annual rings, knots that result from a portion of a tree branch incorporated in cut lumber, and splits which are a separation of the wood due to tearing apart of wood cells. A shake is a lengthwise separation of the wood which usually occurs between the rings of annual growth. None of the above defects should cause you to reject lumber outright. However, wood with a bow, cup, crook, wane, split or twist should be avoided in building construction. Dimensional lumber is typically sold in incremental lengths of 2 feet – for example, 2x6 lumber comes in lengths of 8, 10, 12, 14, 16, and 20 feet. When you plan your shed, you should try to consider standard board lengths in the overall dimensions of your shed. A 12' x 16' shed (192 sq. ft.) will be far more economical to build than a shed measuring 11' x 19' (209 sq. ft.) due to wastage.

The chart at the bottom of page 13 shows you how many studs to purchase for a given length of wall. You should add 2 studs for each corner and 2 extra studs for each door and window.

For example, a 2x6 board measures approximately 1-1/2" x 5-1/2" depending upon moisture content and surface. Lumber that has a rough surface will measure close to the nominal size in comparison to lumber that is surfaced on four sides (known as S4S).

The most critical factor in determining the actual sizes of dimensional lumber is the moisture content of the wood. Look for the grade stamp imprinted on lumber to determine moisture content. Typical moisture content ratings are:

MC 15 (less than 15% moisture content)
S-DRY (less than 19% moisture content)
S-GRN (greater than 19% moisture content)

A 2x6 surfaced unseasoned board (S-GRN) will actually measure 1-9/16" x 5-5/8" compared to 1-1/2" x 5-1/2" for a 2x6 rated surfaced dry (S-DRY). The chart at right shows actual versus nominal sizes of dimensional lumber which is S4S and S-DRY or better. Avoid unseasoned lumber especially in the framing of your shed. Lumber which is unseasoned can shrink considerably as it dries naturally and is certain to cause structural problems as your shed ages.

Choosing the correct lumber for your shed can be as consequential as determining the correct design. For use in a shed, the lumber you select must perform well in an exposed outdoor environment. Performance is measured according to the following criteria:

Freedom from Shrinkage and Warping - Lumber that has dimensional stability will not cause problems later.

Decay Resistance - Generally lumber cut from the heartwood (center of the log) is more resistant to decay than lumber cut from sapwood (outside of the log). However, chemical pressure-treatment can provide decay resistance to species that lack this property.

Workability - Refers to the ease with which you can saw, nail, or shape lumber.

Nail Holding - Determines whether or not a given species possesses good nail-holding power.

Paint Holding - The ability to hold a finish. Some species which contain high levels of natural extractives (such as pitch or resins) do not hold a finish well.

Fire Resistance - All woods are combustible, but some resist fire better than others. Woods that do not contain large amounts of resin are relatively slow to ignite.

Strength and Weight - Wood that is relatively light in weight but possesses great strength is ideal.

Standard Dimensions of Surfaced Lumber

Nominal Size	Surfaced (Actual) Size
1 x 2	3/4" x 1-1/2"
1 x 3	3/4" x 2-1/2"
1 x 4	3/4" x 3-1/2"
1 x 6	3/4" x 5-1/2"
1 x 8	3/4" x 7-1/4"
1 x 10	3/4" x 9-1/4"
1 x 12	3/4" x 11-1/4"
2 x 3	1-1/2" x 2-1/2"
2 x 4	1-1/2" x 3-1/2"
2 x 6	1-1/2" x 5-1/2"
2 x 8	1-1/2" x 7-1/4"
2 x 10	1-1/2" x 9-1/4"
2 x 12	1-1/2" x 11-1/4"
4 x 4	3-1/2" x 3-1/2"
4 x 10	3-1/2" x 9-1/4"
6 x 8	5-1/2" x 7-1/2"

Choosing Lumber for Your Shed

While no single species performs ideally according to all of the criteria above, your local home improvement store or lumber yard will be able to advise you regarding the lumber species most suited to your area. Often you must balance considerations of economy with performance. For example, redwood is considered a premium construction material, but high transportation cost outside the area of manufacture make pressure-treated pine woods a more economical alternative.

Here is a concise guide to some common softwood lumber species used in shed construction:

Cedar, Western Red - Popular for the durability and decay-resistance of its heartwood.

Cypress - Cypress resists decay, has an attractive reddish coloration, and holds paint well.

Douglas Fir, Larch - Douglas Fir has great strength and is used best in the substructure of your deck, especially in the joist members.

Pines - Numerous pine species have excellent workability but must be pressure-treated for use in deck construction.

Southern Pine - Unlike the soft pines described above, southern pines possess strength but are only moderately decay and warp resistant.

Poplar - Has moderate strength, resists decay and warping.

Redwood - The premium decking material because of its durability, resistance to decay, and beautiful natural brownish-red coloration.

Remember that in certain circumstances you can use two different species of lumber to construct your shed. For example, redwood can be used for exterior trim while Douglas Fir is used for strength in the wall and roof framing.

Whatever lumber species you select, it is important to learn the difference between the grain patterns in dimensional lumber. Flat grain lumber is cut with the grain parallel to the face of the board. Typically used for decking, flat grain boards should be used with the bark-side up in order to minimize cupping and grain separation. Vertical grain lumber, a more expensive grade used for finish work, is cut with the grain perpendicular to the face of the board.

Using Engineered Lumber

Due to recent developments in timber cutting practices and the reduced availability of certain sizes of framing lumber, engineered lumber manufactured from plywood, wood chips, and special glue resins offers an attractive alternative to dimensional lumber used for joists, beams, headers, and rafters. Unlike sawn dimensional lumber, engineered lumber is a manufactured product that will not warp and shrink over time.

Engineered lumber is manufactured to meet stringent criteria for strength, uniformity, and reliability (see Figure 13B). Glu-lam beams offer great strength over spans. Wood I-beams provide a lightweight alternative to conventional rafters. Some typical laminated veneer lumber products are shown below.

Figure 13B - Engineered Lumber

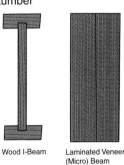

Glu-Lam Beam   Wood I-Beam   Laminated Veneer (Micro) Beam

Figure 13A - Lumber Defects

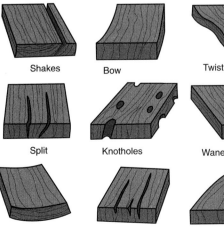

Shakes   Bow   Twist

Split   Knotholes   Wane

Cup   Checks   Crook

Studs Required for Length of Wall

Studs Required for Walls:	Wall Length (in feet)													
	2	3	4	5	6	8	9	10	11	12	14	16	20
16" on center	2	3	4	5	6	6	7	8	9	9	12	13	16
24" on center	2	3	3	4	4	5	5	6	7	7	8	9	11

Ordering Shed Materials

Complete the sample material list below before you begin to shop. If you are using one of the shed plans offered in the back of this manual, each plan comes with a complete list of materials. If you have designed your own shed, create a material list from the final design after approval by your local building department.

Especially consider the quality and grade of the lumber you are purchasing. Poor quality materials will yield a meager return on your shed investment.

Don't hesitate to order at least a 5-10% overage of materials to make up for inevitable cutting mistakes or lumber defects. Be aware that dimensional lumber is sold either by the board foot, the lineal (or running) foot, or by the piece. A board foot of lumber represents the amount of lumber in a board 1" thick x 12' wide x 12' long. Use the following formula to compute board feet:

$$\text{Board Feet} = \frac{\text{Length (Feet) x Width (Inches) x Thickness (Inches)}}{12}$$

Sample Material List

	Size	Length	Quantity X	Cost =	Total Cost
Foundation					
Concrete					
Sand					
Gravel					
Substructure					
Girders					
Skids					
Floor Joists					
Rim Joists					
4' x 8'-3/4" CDX Plywood					
Wall Framing					
Bottom Plates					
Cripple Studs					
Wall Studs					
Top and Tie Plates					
Headers Over Doors					
Headers Over Windows					
Roofing & Siding					
Rafters					
Collar Ties					
Fly Rafters					
Ridge Board					
4' x 8'-1/2" Roof Sheathing					
Roofing Felt					
Self-Sealing Shingles					
4' x 8'-1/2" T1-11 Siding					
Windows & Doors					
Windows					
Doors					
Connectors					
Nails					
Screws					
Bottom Plate to Stud Ties					
Tie Plate to Rafter Ties					
				Grand Total	

Nails and Fasteners

Nails are the most common fastener used in shed framing and construction (see Figure 15). Nail lengths are indicated by the term penny, noted by a small letter **d**. In most cases, nails increase in diameter as they increase in length. Heavier construction framing is accomplished with common nails. The extra thick shank of the common nail has greater strength than other types. A wide thick head spreads the load and resists pull-through. For the substructure and framing of your shed where nails are hidden, consider vinyl coated sinkers or cement coated nails which bond to the wood and will not pull up as readily as uncoated nails.

Box nails are similar in shape to common nails, but they have a slimmer shank that is less likely to split wood. Finishing nails are used in work where you want to counter sink and then cover the nail head.

Roofing nails are essential for attaching roofing materials and preventing moisture penetration through the nail hole.

Screws create neat, strong joists for finished work. Heavy-duty lag screws and lag bolts are useful for heavier framing connections, such as girder-to-post.

Discuss your project with your local home improvement store associate to determine the best nail and fastener selections for your shed project.

Figure 15 - Nails and Fasteners

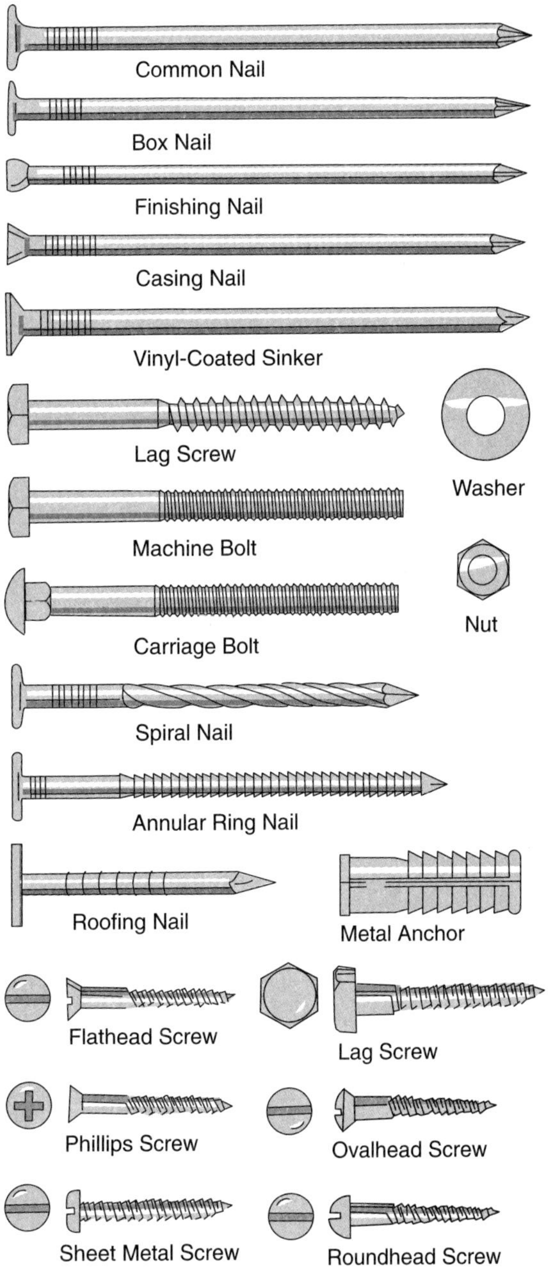

Common Nail
Box Nail
Finishing Nail
Casing Nail
Vinyl-Coated Sinker
Lag Screw
Washer
Machine Bolt
Nut
Carriage Bolt
Spiral Nail
Annular Ring Nail
Roofing Nail
Metal Anchor
Flathead Screw
Lag Screw
Phillips Screw
Ovalhead Screw
Sheet Metal Screw
Roundhead Screw

Table of Common Nails

Size	Length	Gauge	# per lb.
2d	1"	15	840
3d	1 1/4"	14	540
4d	1 1/2"	12 1/2	290
5d	1 3/4"	12 1/2	250
6d	2"	11 1/2	160
7d	2 1/4"	11 1/2	150
8d	2 1/2"	10 1/4	100
9d	2 3/4"	10 1/4	90
10d	3"	9	65
12d	3 1/4"	9	60
16d	3 1/2"	8	45
20d	4"	6	30
30d	4 1/2"	5	20
40d	5"	4	16
50d	5 1/2"	3	12
60d	6"	2	10

Finishing Nail Selection Chart

Size	Length	Gauge	# per lb.
2d	1"	16	1000
3d	1 1/4"	15 1/2	870
4d	1 1/2"	15	600
6d	2"	13	310
8d	2 1/2"	12 1/2	190
10d	3"	11 1/2	120

These tables show the approximate number of nails you get in a pound. You'll need more pounds of larger sizes to do a job. For outside jobs, get galvanized or cadmium-plated nails. Aluminum nails are a bit more expensive unless you are doing a smaller project.

Screw Selection Chart

Size	Length	Size	Length
0	1/4-3/8	9	1/2-3
1	1/4-1/2	10	1/2-3 1/2
2	1/4-3/4	11	5/8-3 1/2
3	1/4-1	12	5/8-4
4	1/4-1 1/2	14	3/4-5
5	3/8-1 1/2	16	1-5
6	3/8-2 1/2	18	1 1/4-5
7	3/8-2 1/2	20	1 1/2-5
8	3/8-3	24	3-5

The screw chart shows sizes and the lengths in which they're available. The larger sizes come in longer lengths. Most jobs call for sizes 6-12 in 1/2 to 3 inch lengths. Check size & length before you buy.

Framing with Metal Fasteners

A wide variety of metal fasteners are available to make your shed sturdy and long-lasting (see Figure 16). You may be required by local codes to add seismic and hurricane connectors to each stud where it connects to the bottom and top plate. Rafter and tie plate connectors offer a quick method of attaching the roof rafters to the tie plate without making a bird's mouth cut. Nail-on plates can replace plywood gussets in gambrel roof construction and help to create a rigid roof frame. Be sure to follow the manufacturer's installation instructions.

Figure 16 - Variety of Metal Fasteners

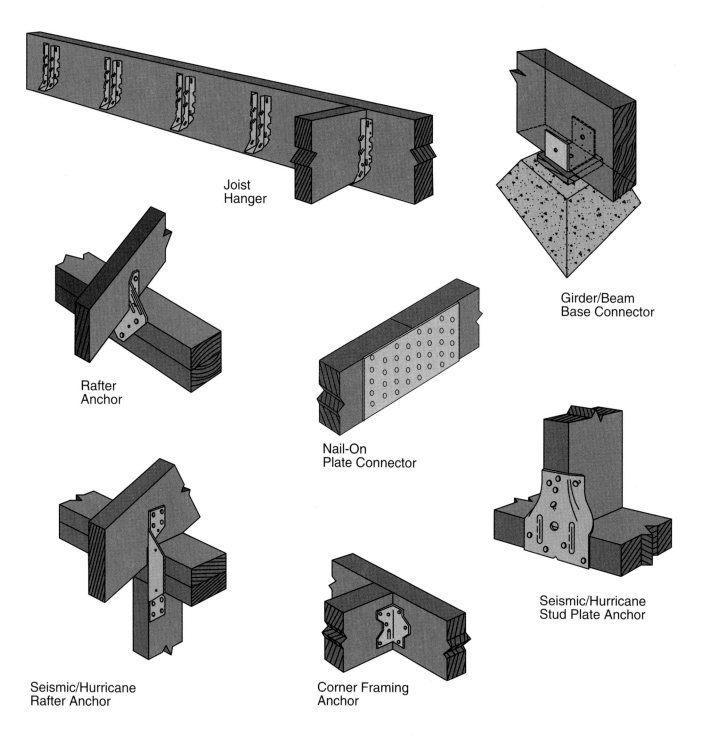

Joist Hanger

Girder/Beam Base Connector

Rafter Anchor

Nail-On Plate Connector

Seismic/Hurricane Stud Plate Anchor

Seismic/Hurricane Rafter Anchor

Corner Framing Anchor

Framing with Metal Fasteners

Right-angled corner framing anchors add strength to perpendicular butt joints, especially where rim joists meet. Use joist hangers to attach your floor joists to rim joist members. Beam connectors provide a strong connection between beams and posts or pier blocks. The modest additional expense of metal fasteners will be more than offset by the added durability of your shed. Secure fasteners using the short ribbed nails provided or where extra strength is required use lag screws in addition to nails.

Figure 17A - Girder/Beam Frame Connector

Available sizes for:
2x4 Joists
2x6 Joists

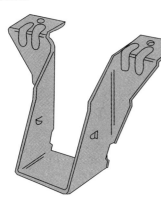 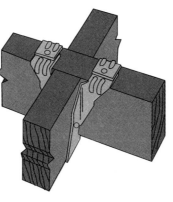 

Figure 17B - Variety of Connectors

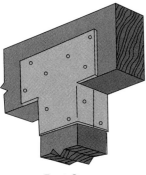 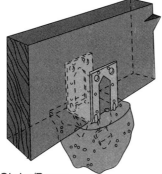 

Post Cap
Connector

Girder/Beam
Base Connector

Plywood
Sheathing Clips

Figure 17C - Adjustable Post Anchor

Available sizes for:
4x4 Posts
4x6 Posts
6x6 Posts

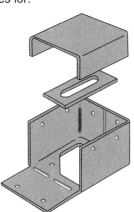 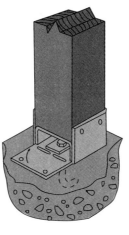 

Typical Shed Floor Plan

Floor Framing Plan

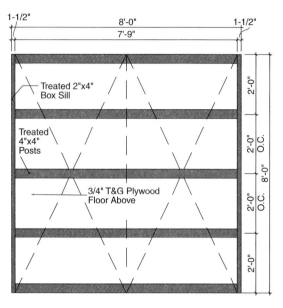

- 1-1/2"
- 8'-0"
- 7'-9"
- 1-1/2"
- 2'-0"
- 2'-0"
- 8'-0" O.C.
- 2'-0" O.C.
- 2'-0"

Treated 2"x4" Box Sill

Treated 4"x4" Posts

3/4" T&G Plywood Floor Above

Floor Plan

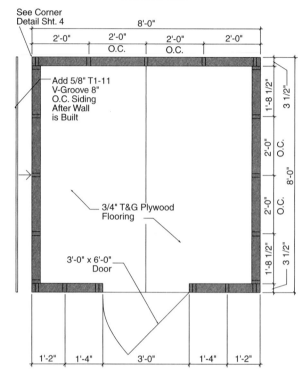

See Corner Detail Sht. 4

Add 5/8" T1-11 V-Groove 8" O.C. Siding After Wall is Built

3/4" T&G Plywood Flooring

3'-0" x 6'-0" Door

- 8'-0"
- 2'-0"
- 2'-0" O.C.
- 2'-0" O.C.
- 2'-0"
- 1'-8 1/2"
- 3 1/2"
- 2'-0" O.C.
- 8'-0" O.C.
- 2'-0" O.C.
- 1'-8 1/2"
- 3 1/2"
- 1'-2"
- 1'-4"
- 3'-0"
- 1'-4"
- 1'-2"

Typical Wall and Roof Framing Plan

Rear Wall Framing Plan

Side Wall Framing Plan

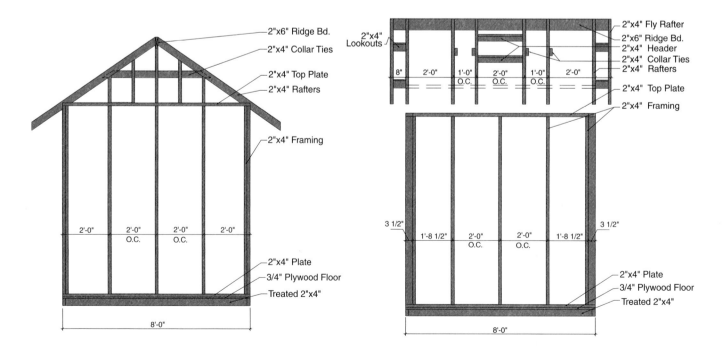

Rear Wall Framing Plan labels:
- 2"x6" Ridge Bd.
- 2"x4" Collar Ties
- 2"x4" Top Plate
- 2"x4" Rafters
- 2"x4" Framing
- 2"x4" Plate
- 3/4" Plywood Floor
- Treated 2"x4"
- 2'-0"
- 2'-0" O.C.
- 2'-0" O.C.
- 2'-0"
- 8'-0"

Side Wall Framing Plan labels:
- 2"x4" Lookouts
- 2"x4" Fly Rafter
- 2"x6" Ridge Bd.
- 2"x4" Header
- 2"x4" Collar Ties
- 2"x4" Rafters
- 2"x4" Top Plate
- 2"x4" Framing
- 2"x4" Plate
- 3/4" Plywood Floor
- Treated 2"x4"
- 8"
- 2'-0"
- 1'-0" O.C.
- 2'-0" O.C.
- 1'-0" O.C.
- 2'-0"
- 3 1/2"
- 1'-8 1/2"
- 2'-0" O.C.
- 2'-0" O.C.
- 1'-8 1/2"
- 3 1/2"
- 8'-0"

Constructing the Basic Wall Frame

To begin, cut both the top and bottom plates to length. In most cases, you will need more than one piece of lumber for each plate. So locate the joints at stud centers and offset joints between top and bottom plates by at least 4'-0" (see Figure 19).

Lay the top plate against the bottom plate on the floor as illustrated below. Beginning at one end, measure 15-1/4" in and draw a line across both plates. Measure out farther along the plates an additional distance of 1-1/2" from this line, and draw a second line. The first interior stud will be placed between these lines. From these lines, advance 16" at a time, drawing new lines, until you reach the far end of the plates. Each set of lines will outline the placement of a stud with all studs evenly spaced at 16" on center. If you are using studs on 24" centers, the first measurement in from the edge would be 23-1/4".

Assembling the Pieces

If you are using precut studs (either 92-1/4" or 92-5/8" in length), no cutting is required. Otherwise measure and cut the wall studs to exact length. Position the plates apart on the floor and turn them on edge with the stud marking toward the center. Place the studs between the lines and nail them through each plate with two 16d common nails.

Framing Corners

Where walls meet, you might need extra studs to handle the corner tie to the adjacent wall. These extra studs should be added to the ends of the longer two of the four walls. The exact positioning of these extra corner studs is shown at the bottom of page 23.

Figure 19 - Assembling the Wall Frame

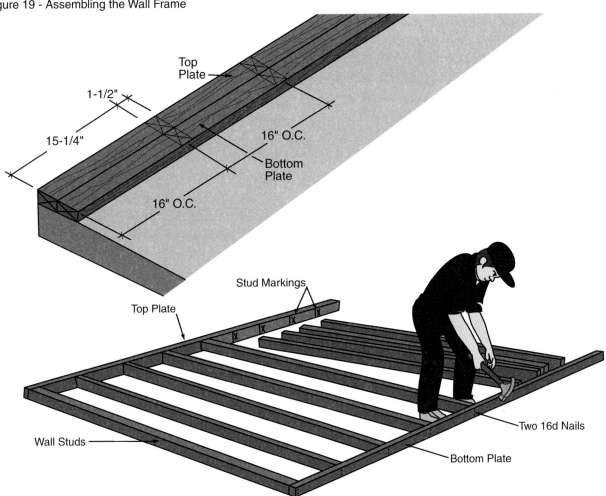

Door and Window Framing

At door and window openings there is no stud support, so a header is required. Door and window headers can be constructed either from 4x dimensional lumber, veneer laminate lumber also known as engineered lumber, or two lengths of 2x material on edge with a 1/2" piece of plywood sandwiched between them (see Figure 20A). When you are constructing a built-up header from doubled-up 2x material, the plywood makes the header the same 3-1/2" width as the studs.

Headers are always installed on edge as shown. Consult the chart below to determine the header size required for a given span.

The spaces above door openings and above and below windows are framed with cripple studs spaced 16" on center (see Figure 20B). Study the illustrations to become familiar with the king and trimmer stud locations used in framing doors and windows.

The rough framed door should be 1-1/2" higher than the usual 80" actual door height and 2-1/2" wider than the door to account for doorjamb material. When the 1-1/2" bottom plate is cut from the opening, this adds the needed 1-1/2" in extra height.

In addition to cripple studs, king studs, and trimmer studs, window framing also uses a rough sill to support the window. Headers should be set at the same time as door headers. Consult the manufacturer's instructions for a suggested rough-out opening to accommodate a given window.

Header Assembly

Nail two pieces of 2xs and plywood to the length between king studs with 16d nails spaced 16" apart along both top and bottom edges.

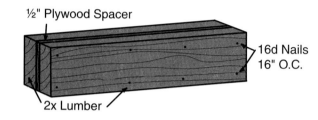

Figure 20A - Header Assembly

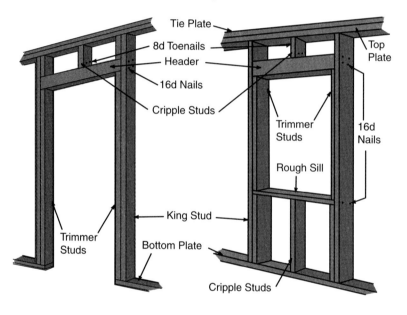

Figure 20B - Door and Window Framing

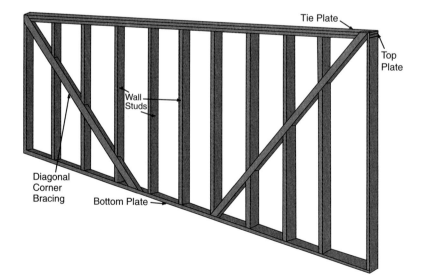

Figure 20C - Wall Framing

Header Size (4x or built-up 2x)	Maximum Span (feet)
4 x 4	4'
4 x 6	6'
4 x 8	8'
4 x 10	10'
4 x 12	12'

Diagonal Bracing

Structures with plywood siding do not normally require bracing, but all others do. The two most commonly used types of bracing are wooden "let-in" bracing made of 1x4 stock and metal strap bracing.

Let-in Bracing

This type of wooden bracing runs from the top outside corners of the wall to the bottom center of the wall (see Figure 21A). It forms a V-shaped configuration as shown on page 20. These braces are set into notched studs and are prepared while the wall frame is still lying on the slab.

Lay the 1x4 on the frame with one end at a top corner and the other end as far out on the bottom plate as possible without running into any door or window opening. Mark the underside of the brace where it overhangs the top and bottom plates to determine the angle at which the plates cross. Also mark both sides of the studs and plates at each point the brace crosses them. Notch the studs at these locations by making repeated cuts with your circular saw. Use a hammer and wood chisel to knock out any stubborn chips. Trim the ends of the 1x4 and put the brace in place. Hold it in place with a single nail until the wall is raised and plumbed. Then nail the brace fast with 8d nails wherever it crosses a plate or stud.

Metal Strap Bracing

Commonly available in 10' to 12' lengths, this type of bracing is nailed to the outside of the studded walls after they are raised, square, and plumb (see Figure 21B). Metal bracing is thin enough not to obstruct the exterior wall sheathing.

The straps have predrilled holes every 2" sized to accept an 8d nail. Strap bracing must always be installed in crossed pairs, similar to a large X design.

Figure 21B - Alternative Metal Strap

Figure 21A - Bracing

Step 1 - Mark bracing locations.

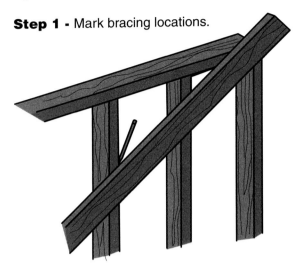

Step 2 - Notch out studs.

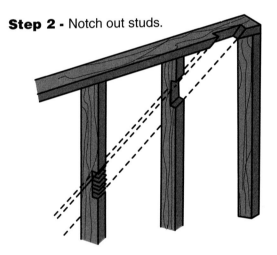

Step 3 - Nail bracing into stud locations.

Raising the Walls

Most walls can be raised by hand if enough help is available on the job site. It is advisable to have one person for every 10' of wall for the lifting operation.

The order in which walls are framed and raised can vary from job to job, but in general, the longer exterior walls are framed first. The shorter exterior walls are then raised and the corners are nailed together.

Once the first wall is framed out, there are only a few short steps until it is up and standing. If you are raising a wall on a slab, slide the wall along the slab until the bottom plate lies near the anchor bolt at the floor's edge. If you are raising a wall on a wood floor, you might want to tack some scrap lumber along the floor rim joists to prevent the wall from slipping over the edge. To raise the wall, you should have your workers grip it at the top plate in unison and work their hands beneath the plate (see Figure 22). Now everyone walks down the wall until it is in the upright position. On a slab you need to slip the bottom plate in place over the anchor bolts as you tilt the wall up.

To brace the wall, tack 2x4 braces to the wall studs, one at each end and one in the middle if the wall is particularly long. Tie these braces into stakes driven firmly into the ground or tack them to the wood floor rim joists if appropriate. Secure the wall by using washers and nuts if you have anchor bolts or tack the bottom plate to the wood floor. Do not securely nail the bottom plate to the floor until you are certain that the wall is in proper alignment.

To check alignment, use a carpenter's level to check the wall for plumb along both end studs on adjacent faces. If the wall is out of plumb, loosen that brace, align the wall, and secure the brace again. If an end stud is warped, bridge the warp with a straight board. When both ends are plumb, adjust the middle.

Nailing Schedule for Structural Members

Description of Building Materials	Number & Type of Fastener	Spacing of Fasteners
Top or sole plate to stud, end nail	2-16d	-
Stud to sole plate, toenail	4-8d or 3-16d	-
Doubled studs, face nail	16d	24" O.C.
Doubled top plates, face nail	16d	16" O.C.
Top plates, taps and intersections, face nail	2-16d	-
Continued header, two pieces	16d	16" O.C. along each edge
Ceiling joists to plate, toenail	2-16d	-
Continuous header to stud, toenail	4-8d	-
Ceiling joist, taps over partitions, face nail	3-16d	-
Ceiling joist to parallel rafters, face nail	3-16d	-
Rafter to plate, toenail	2-16d	-
1" brace to each stud and plate, face nail	2-8d	-
Built-up corner studs	16d	30" O.C.
Built-up girder and beams	16d	32" O.C. at top & bottom & staggered 2-20d at ends & at each splice
Roof rafters to ridge, valley or hip rafters, toe nail	4-16d	-
Face nail	3-16d	-
Collar ties to rafters, face nail	3-8d	-

Description of Building Materials	Description of Fasteners	Spacing of Fasteners
Roof and wall sheathing to frame		
1/2 inch to 5/16 inch roof & wall sheathing to frame	6d	6" edges 12" intermediate supports
Other wall sheathing		
1/2 inch fiberboard sheathing	1 1/2" galvanized roofing nail 6d common nail	3" edges 6" intermediate supports

Figure 22 - To raise the wall, have your workers grip it at the top plate in unison and work their hands beneath the plate. Now everyone walks until it is in the upright position.

To check alignment, use a carpenter's level.

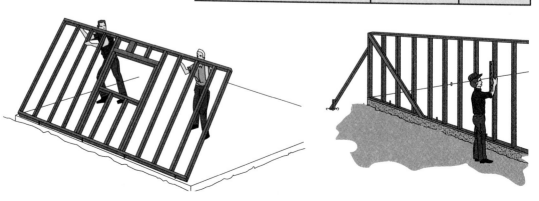

Once raised, the wall should also be checked for levelness. If needed, it can be shimmed level using tapered cedar shingles driven between the foundation and the bottom plate. Once the wall is plumb and level, tighten the anchor nuts to their final tightness or on wooden floors nail two 16d common nails between each stud. Do not nail the bottom plate in a door opening since this section must be cut out for the door.

At corners, nail through the end walls into the stud using 16d common nails staggered every 12". When the walls are up, you can then add the 2x4 tie plates to the top plates on each wall. These tie plates lap over onto adjacent walls to interlock the walls and give added strength to the structure.

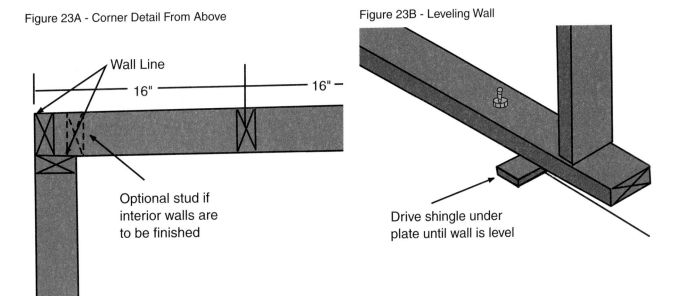

Figure 23A - Corner Detail From Above

Wall Line

16"

16"

Optional stud if interior walls are to be finished

Figure 23B - Leveling Wall

Drive shingle under plate until wall is level

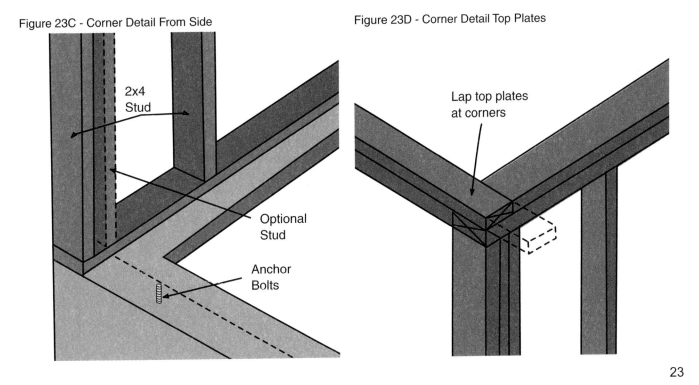

Figure 23C - Corner Detail From Side

2x4 Stud

Optional Stud

Anchor Bolts

Figure 23D - Corner Detail Top Plates

Lap top plates at corners

Roof Framing

Most roof designs are variations of the gable roof, in which evenly spaced pairs of common rafters join the tie plates and central ridge board together. A hip roof is also used in shed construction and most often utilizes small hip roof trusses to create the roof framing. Rafters are 2x4s, 2x6s, or 2x8s depending upon span, spacing, load, and roof slope. They are installed on 16" or 24" centers. Check with your local building department for help regarding rafter requirements and roof load in your area. At the peak, rafter boards butt against a central ridge board. The ridge board can be either 1x or 2x lumber and is one size wider than the rafter lumber. Slope, or pitch, is referred to in terms of unit rise in a given unit run. Unit run is fixed at 12 inches. Unit rise is the slope over those 12 inches. A rise of 4" over 12" equals a slope of 4 in 12".

Cutting the Rafters

A common rafter has three cuts: the plumb cut to form the angle where the rafter meets the ridge board, the bird's mouth notch to fit the top plate, and the tail cut at the end of the overhang. Professionally prepared plans often have a template or diagram that serves as a master for rafter cutting. Cut two rafters off the master and check them for accuracy before using the others. Use a steel carpenter's square to mark the cuts.

Raising the Roof

With ridge board and rafters cut, you can raise the roof. Unless the roof is small, you'll need three people. Nail an upright 2x4 for each of the end rafters flush against the middle of the end top plate. One person then lines up one end rafter with the end of the side top plate and ties it in with three 16d nails. The second raises and holds it at the correct slope against one of the 2x4s, while the third tacks the two together. Do the same with the opposite end rafter, then align the ridge board between the top of the rafters and tie it in with three 16d common nails through each rafter. Use 8d common nails if the ridge board is 1x common lumber. The ridge board must be level, and the rafter ends must be flush with the sides of the ridge board. Repeat the process at the opposite end for a single-piece ridge board. For a two-piece ridge board, connect the rafters to the last spacing mark at the opposite end.

Figure 24 - For those of us not familiar with a square, lay out the initial pair of rafters on the slab. Snap chalk lines to represent the bottom of the rafters and the plate line. Use the rise in 12" to establish the angle (for example, 4" in 12"). If they fit, use them as patterns for all other rafters.

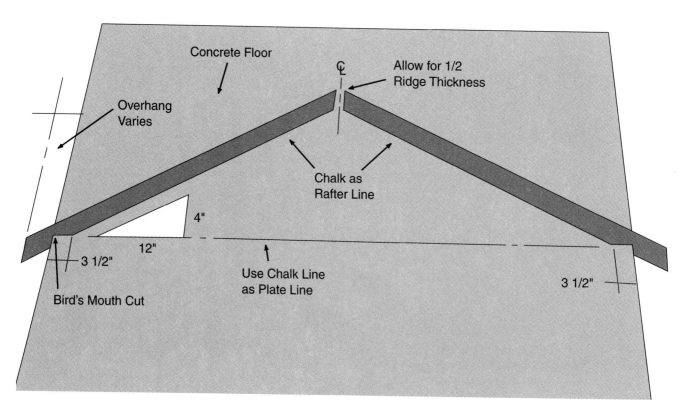

Roof Framing

Figure 25A - Typical Storage Building Section
(for reference only)

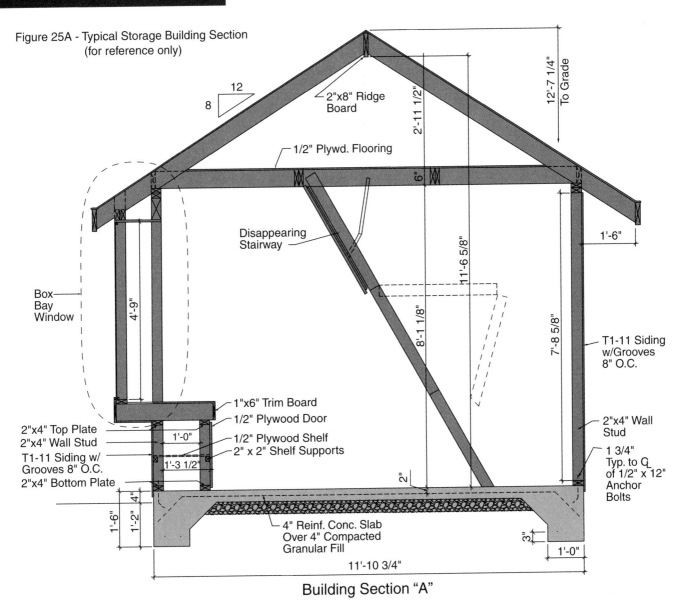

Building Section "A"

12
8

2"x8" Ridge Board

12'-7 1/4" To Grade

2'-11 1/2"

1/2" Plywd. Flooring

6"

1'-6"

Disappearing Stairway

11'-6 5/8"

8'-1 1/8"

7'-8 5/8"

T1-11 Siding w/Grooves 8" O.C.

Box Bay Window

4'-9"

2"x4" Wall Stud

1 3/4" Typ. to Ç of 1/2" x 12" Anchor Bolts

1"x6" Trim Board
1/2" Plywood Door
1/2" Plywood Shelf
2" x 2" Shelf Supports

2"x4" Top Plate
2"x4" Wall Stud
T1-11 Siding w/ Grooves 8" O.C.
2"x4" Bottom Plate

1'-0"

1'-3 1/2"

2"

4"

2"

1'-6"
1'-2"

4" Reinf. Conc. Slab Over 4" Compacted Granular Fill

3"

1'-0"

11'-10 3/4"

Figure 25B - Typical Rafter Cutting Diagram

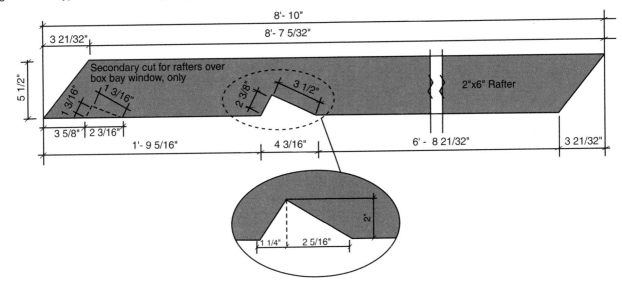

8'- 10"
8'- 7 5/32"
3 21/32"
5 1/2"
1 3/16"   1 3/16"
3 5/8"   2 3/16"
1'- 9 5/16"
Secondary cut for rafters over box bay window, only
2 3/8"   3 1/2"
4 3/16"
2"x6" Rafter
6'- 8 21/32"
3 21/32"

2"
1 1/4"   2 5/16"

25

Erecting the Rafters

Make sure the end rafters are plumb and that the ridge board is level and centered mid-span. Next attach a diagonal brace between the ridge board and the 2x4 nailed to the top plate. Run the remaining rafters in pairs, attaching them to the ridge board first, then to the top plate (see Figures 26A - B). If your local codes require seismic/hurricane anchors, use metal connectors to secure the rafters to the top plate.

If a second ridge board is used, the process is repeated from the opposite end of the building. The junction of the ridge boards must be covered by two rafters. If you plan to install rafter ties (or ceiling joists), use three 16d nails to tie rafters to the rafter ties and cut the ties to match the slope of the rafters.

Be sure to add collar ties and hangers before removing any shoring or bracing.

Figure 26A - Ridge Board Supports

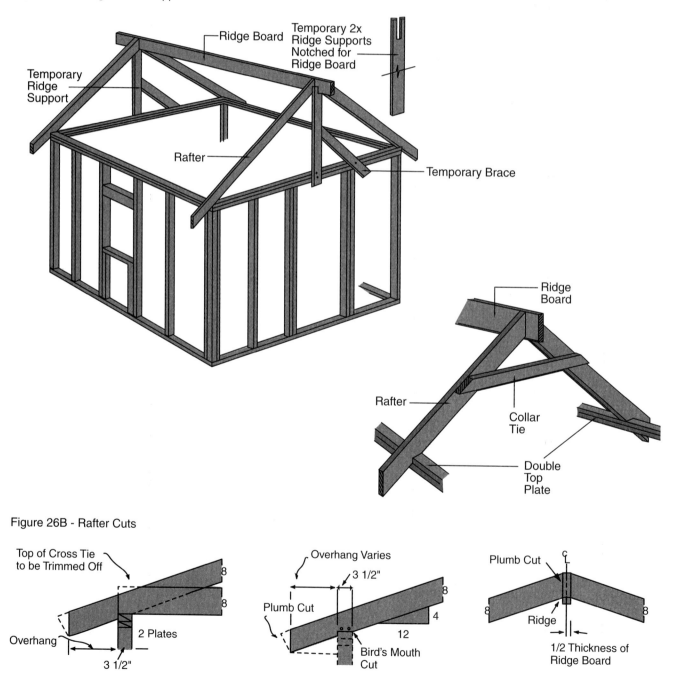

Figure 26B - Rafter Cuts

Using Metal Connectors For Framing

As mentioned earlier, metal fasteners provide the strength nails alone cannot provide. They also avoid the irritation of watching angled nails split the lumber that you have so carefully cut and fitted. Certain metal connectors allow the rafter to rest directly on the tie or top plate and eliminate the difficult and time-consuming bird's mouth cut (see Figure 27).

Other connectors are designed to join the rafter to the ridge board without toenailing. As you can see from the illustrations below, many different types of metal connectors are available for roof framing work. While metal roof framing connectors will add some additional expense to your project, they will save you time and create a more durable shed.

Figure 27 - Rafter Connector Examples

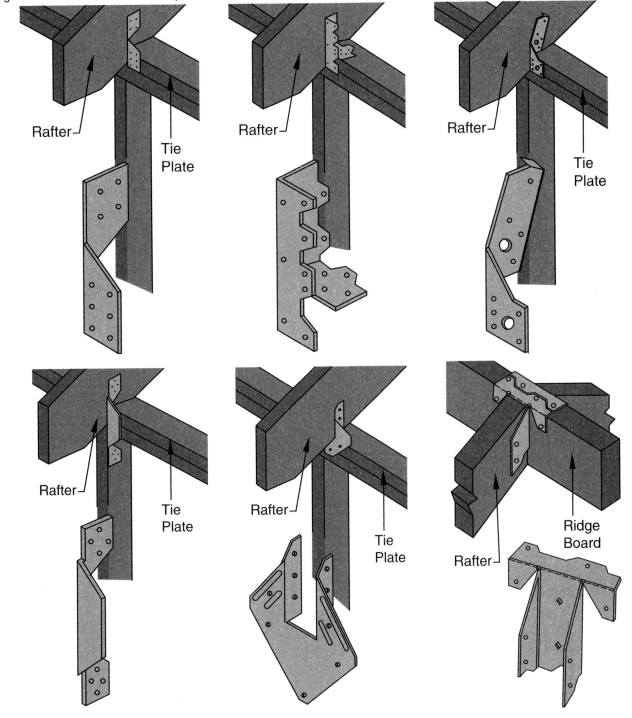

Variations of the Roof Cornice

Whatever type of roof you decide to construct, your building will have a roof overhang to protect the top of the side walls from moisture penetration. This overhang is generally known as the roof cornice. The cornice can also serve to provide ventilation and protection from the hot overhead rays of the sun on the sidewalls. As a general rule of thumb, warmer climates tend to favor longer overhangs that offer greater shading.

An open cornice is illustrated in Figure 28A. The overhang can extend up to 24" from the edge of the building. You have the option of adding a frieze board to the rafter ends or leaving the rafter ends exposed. Remember that when you create an exposed overhang, the roof sheathing is visible from underneath. Painting or staining the sheathing can improve its appearance.

Figure 28B represents a closed cornice. Make a seat cut on the rafter at the top plate. Cut the rafter ends flush and vertical with the top plate. Bring the siding all the way up to the rafters and finish off the cornice with a trim piece that covers the slightly exposed roof sheathing.

Two variations of the boxed cornice are shown in Figures 28C and 28D. A fascia board at the rafter ends is essential for any style of boxed cornice. Figure 28C demonstrates the sloping soffit design where the rafters are used to directly attach the soffit board. Nail a 1x fascia to the square cut rafter ends. Another frieze board covers the end portion of the soffit where it meets the wall siding.

Figure 28D portrays the level soffit design that requires 2x4 horizontal lookouts facenailed at the rafter ends and toenailed to wall siding. Level soffits generally extend no more than 12"-15" from the building wall. The lookouts help to frame the soffit construction.

Proper ventilation is essential for the boxed cornice. Install soffit vents (typically 4"x8") at regular intervals along the soffit between the lookouts. Be sure to install the screened vents or you will have unintentionally created a birdhouse wherever you have an unscreened vent!

Ventilation

If you plan to use your shed as a work area where you will spend longer periods of time, consider installing either gable end vents or roof vents. Vents help to reduce interior temperatures during the summer and to minimize condensation during the winter months. Gable end vents should be installed at both gable ends of your roof to promote cross-ventilation.

The number of roof vents you will install depends upon the cubic footage of your building. Simply create a box frame between roof rafters and install the vent according to the manufacturer's instructions. Don't forget to flash and then caulk the vent after you have installed the roof sheathing and shingles.

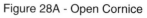
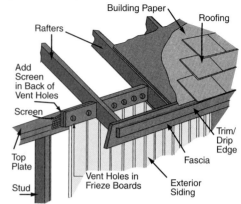

Figure 28A - Open Cornice

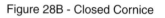
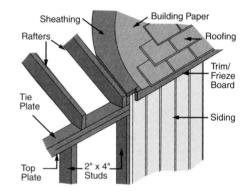

Figure 28B - Closed Cornice

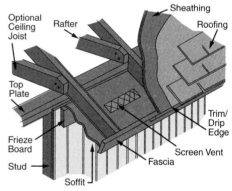

Figure 28C - Boxed Cornice/Sloping Soffit

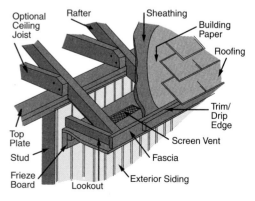

Figure 28D - Boxed Cornice/Level Soffit

Roof Sheathing

Use 4'x8' plywood roof sheathing panels to create a strong base for your roofing material. The required thickness of sheathing will vary with rafter spacing and local building code requirements. Generally, the wider the rafter spacing, the thicker the sheathing needs to be. If you want the interior of your shed to have a finished building look, use 2x6 tongue and groove material to create a solid roof sheathing and paint the underside.

Stagger the sheathing, starting at the bottom, so that the end joints of adjacent sheets fall on different rafters. Space 6d nails 6" apart at sheet ends and 12" on center at intermediate rafters. Leave a 1/16" expansion gap between the ends of sheets. For larger jobs, you might want to rent a pneumatic staple gun to fasten sheathing. If gable eaves have an overhang, be certain to extend the sheathing to cover it.

Figure 29 - Plywood Sheathing Layout Plan

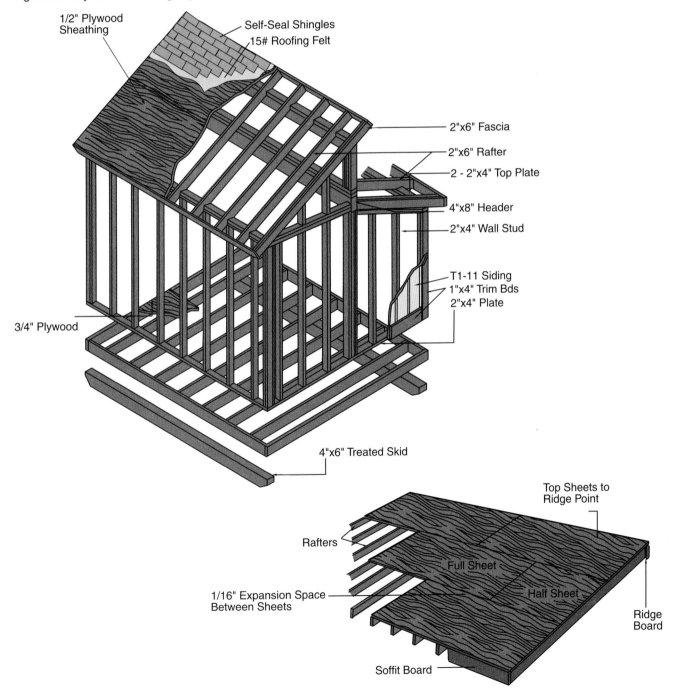

1/2" Plywood Sheathing

Self-Seal Shingles
15# Roofing Felt

2"x6" Fascia

2"x6" Rafter

2 - 2"x4" Top Plate

4"x8" Header

2"x4" Wall Stud

T1-11 Siding
1"x4" Trim Bds
2"x4" Plate

3/4" Plywood

4"x6" Treated Skid

Top Sheets to Ridge Point

Rafters

Full Sheet

Half Sheet

1/16" Expansion Space Between Sheets

Ridge Board

Soffit Board

Roof Framing

Gambrel Roof Construction

The gambrel roof offers an attractive barn-like alternative for shed design. Construct gambrel roof framing from trusses built on the ground and then erect the relatively lightweight trusses over the wall framing.

To add additional strength to your gambrel roof trusses in areas with heavy snow loads, use truss plate connectors and truss tie-down brackets to connect the truss to the top plate.

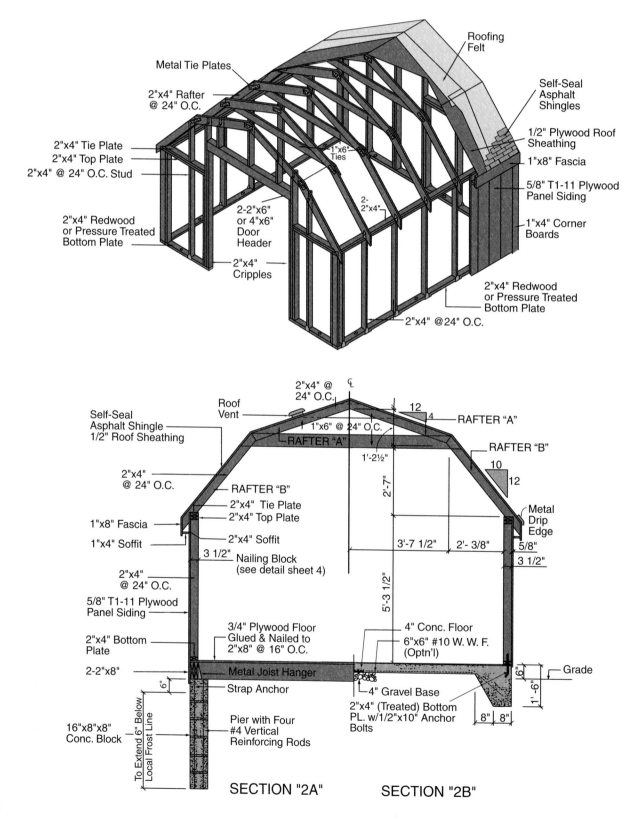

Metal Tie Plates

2"x4" Rafter @ 24" O.C.

2"x4" Tie Plate
2"x4" Top Plate
2"x4" @ 24" O.C. Stud

2"x4" Redwood or Pressure Treated Bottom Plate

2-2"x6" or 4"x6" Door Header

2"x4" Cripples

Roofing Felt

Self-Seal Asphalt Shingles

1/2" Plywood Roof Sheathing

1"x8" Fascia

5/8" T1-11 Plywood Panel Siding

1"x4" Corner Boards

2"x4" Redwood or Pressure Treated Bottom Plate

2"x4" @ 24" O.C.

1"x6" Ties

2-2"x4"

Self-Seal Asphalt Shingle
1/2" Roof Sheathing

Roof Vent

2"x4" @ 24" O.C.

1"x6" @ 24" O.C.

RAFTER "A"

12
4

RAFTER "A"

RAFTER "B"

2"x4" @ 24" O.C.

RAFTER "B"

2"x4" Tie Plate
2"x4" Top Plate

2"x4" Soffit

1"x8" Fascia

1"x4" Soffit

3 1/2" Nailing Block (see detail sheet 4)

2"x4" @ 24" O.C.

5/8" T1-11 Plywood Panel Siding

2"x4" Bottom Plate

2-2"x8"

16"x8"x8" Conc. Block

To Extend 6" Below Local Frost Line

6"

Strap Anchor

Pier with Four #4 Vertical Reinforcing Rods

3/4" Plywood Floor Glued & Nailed to 2"x8" @ 16" O.C.

Metal Joist Hanger

1'-2½"

2'-7"

5'-3 1/2"

3'-7 1/2"   2'- 3/8"

10
12

Metal Drip Edge

5/8"

3 1/2"

4" Conc. Floor
6"x6" #10 W. W. F. (Optn'l)

4" Gravel Base

2"x4" (Treated) Bottom PL. w/1/2"x10" Anchor Bolts

6"

Grade

1'- 6"

8" 8"

SECTION "2A"

SECTION "2B"

Roof Framing

Shed Roof Construction

The shed roof lowers the height of one wall to create a lean-to appearance. Shed roofing is typical for buildings with clerestory windows like the design illustrated below. The advantage of the shed roof and clerestory window combination is that without wall windows all of your wall space is available for storage but you still have plenty of natural lighting provided by the windows above your workspace.

Figure 31 - Section With Window Lighting

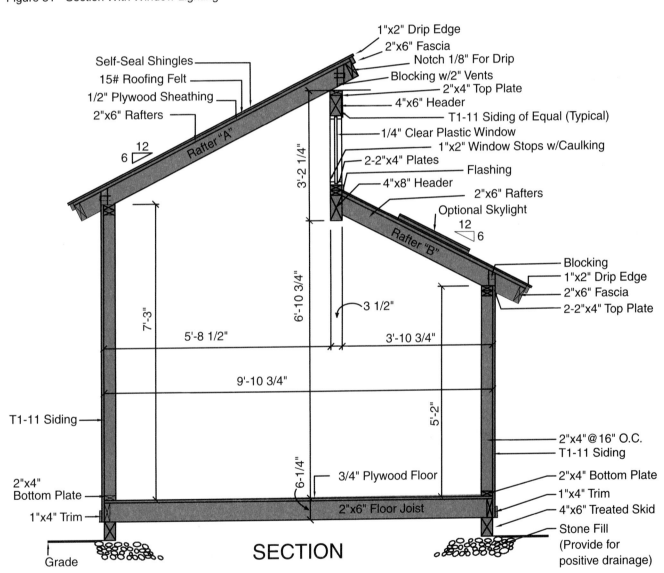

SECTION

Applying Vertical Panel Siding

Before starting construction, select the siding and determine the need for wall sheathing. Wall sheathing requirements are determined by the stud spacing, the width of the door and window jambs, and the application of the trim (see Figure 32A).

A commonplace and inexpensive siding for sheds, T1-11 exterior siding does not require wall sheathing and adds structural strength. Flakeboard (Oriented Strand Board) is another inexpensive siding option for those with a tight budget. When you install vertical panel siding, nail 6d galvanized nails every 4"-6" at the edges of the panel and every 8"-12" inside the panel. You might be able to obtain siding nails that match the siding and thus eliminate painting both the siding and nails. If you have to add a panel above the bottom panel, use Z-bar flashing between the panels (see Figure 32C). Leave a 1/4" gap around door and window openings when cutting siding to facilitate fitting.

When plywood sheathing is used, diagonal corner bracing can often be omitted. Decide whether trim is to be applied on top of the siding or butted into it. If butted, apply trim first, then apply siding. Horizontal wood siding is more expensive than plywood panel siding but provides an attractive and durable exterior. However, horizontal wood siding requires periodic painting for preservation.

Figure 32A - Siding Alternatives

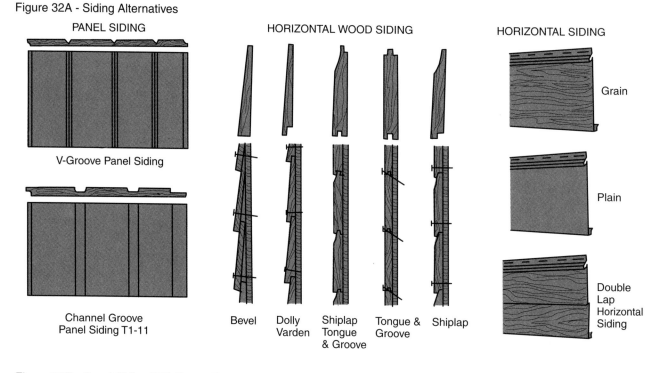

PANEL SIDING

V-Groove Panel Siding

Channel Groove Panel Siding T1-11

HORIZONTAL WOOD SIDING

Bevel Dolly Varden Shiplap Tongue & Groove Tongue & Groove Shiplap

HORIZONTAL SIDING

Grain

Plain

Double Lap Horizontal Siding

Figure 32B - Panel Siding With Batten Boards

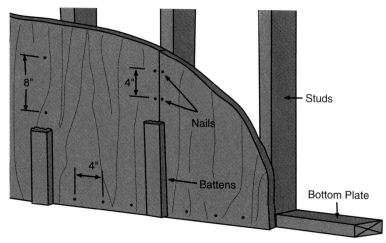

8" 4" 4"

Nails

Studs

Battens

Bottom Plate

Figure 32C - Vertical Grooved Siding Panels

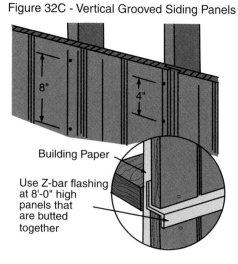

8" 4"

Building Paper

Use Z-bar flashing at 8'-0" high panels that are butted together

Applying Horizontal Hardboard Siding

Lay down various lengths of siding at each side. Apply so that joints in the succeeding course do not fall directly above each other. Butt all joints over the center of a stud. Seal by painting the edges with primer before butting. Start the bottom of the first course 1/2" below the bottom plate. Siding on all walls should be aligned and level and each course equally spaced. Be especially careful to determine the lap and exposure to the weather before applying the second and succeeding courses. Measure the distance to be covered and divide it by the desired exposure to get the total number of courses of siding. See Figure 33A below. Carefully mark these spaces on the corners of each wall, taking into consideration the overlap of the siding. Run a chalk line from one mark to another, leaving a horizontal chalk line on the building paper as a guide. If you are not applying sheathing or building paper, chalk the wall studs directly. Apply the siding and keep it consistent by checking your level.

Final openings, where siding meets the soffit if applicable, can be closed with a piece of quarter round or shingle mould. Protect your shed by painting or staining it as soon as possible.

Figure 33A - Marking Siding Courses

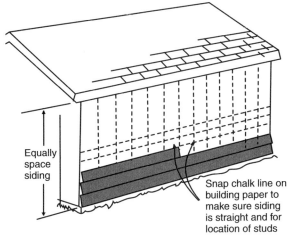

Equally space siding

Snap chalk line on building paper to make sure siding is straight and for location of studs

Figure 33B - Horizontal Siding Detail

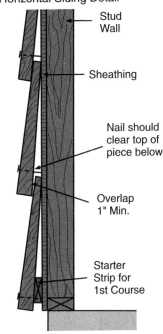

Stud Wall

Sheathing

Nail should clear top of piece below

Overlap 1" Min.

Starter Strip for 1st Course

Building Paper

Some local building codes might require that building paper be used to seal the wall from the elements. Building paper is typically felt or kraft paper impregnated with asphalt and is stapled or nailed between the siding and the sheathing or studs. Rolls are usually 36" wide and come in lengths covering between 200 to 500 square feet. Apply building paper in horizontal strips from the bottom of the wall as shown in Figure 33C. Overlaps should be 2" at horizontal joints, 6" at vertical joints, and 12" at corners. Cutting is done with a utility knife. Use just enough staples or nails in an installation to hold the paper in place. Siding nails will hold it permanently. Before you install siding, snap a level chalk line on the siding to indicate the bottom edge of the paper and work up.

Figure 33C - Applying Building Paper

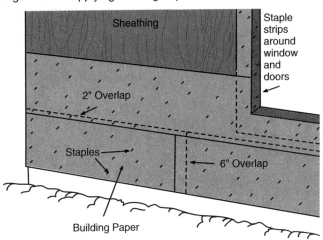

Sheathing

Staple strips around window and doors

2" Overlap

Staples

6" Overlap

Building Paper

Overhang Details

Before applying trim, know the nailing requirements of the siding you select. Some siding will have trim applied over the siding, but other siding will butt against trim and require extra blocking at the edges. After the roof sheathing is on but before you install the fascia and rake boards, add soffit nailers if required. Use the longest fascia boards on the longest walls. Join all ends over the center of a rafter or nailer. Consult Figures 34A to 34F below. At the gable end, extend the fascia (or rake board) along the edge of the roof sheathing and rafter. At the top, cut the end to the angle of the rafter and butt at the center. Be sure to prime coat both ends before butting. At the lower end, let the front rake fascia extend beyond the side fascia, then cut the ends to line up with the side fascia.

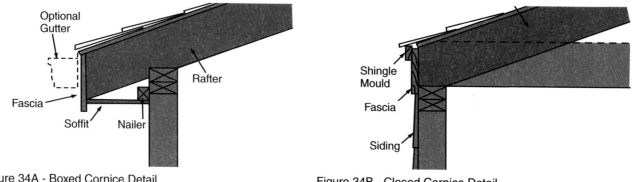

Figure 34A - Boxed Cornice Detail

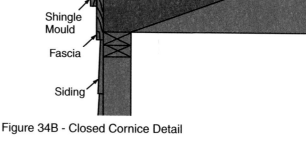

Figure 34B - Closed Cornice Detail

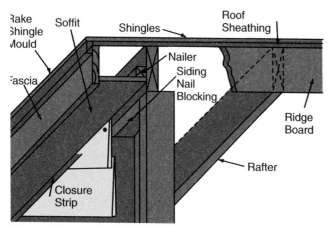

Figure 34C - Gable End Ridge Detail Box Overhang

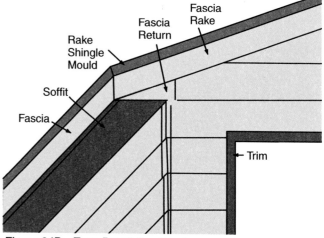

Figure 34D - Eave Detail Box Overhang

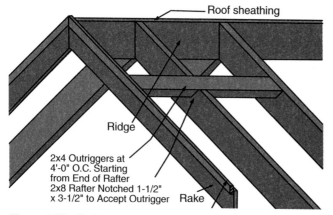

Figure 34E - Gable End Ridge Detail Open Overhang

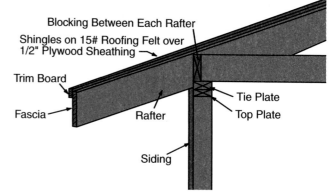

Figure 34F - Open Cornice Overhang

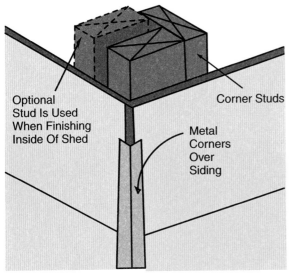

Optional Stud Is Used When Finishing Inside Of Shed

Corner Studs

Metal Corners Over Siding

Figure 35A - Corner Tins

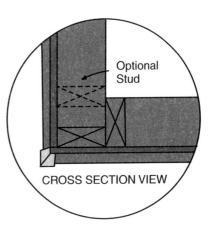

Optional Stud

CROSS SECTION VIEW

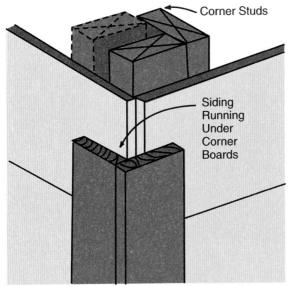

Corner Studs

Siding Running Under Corner Boards

Figure 35B - Corner Boards

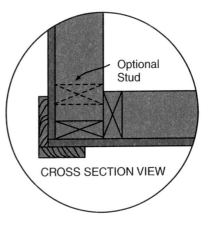

Optional Stud

CROSS SECTION VIEW

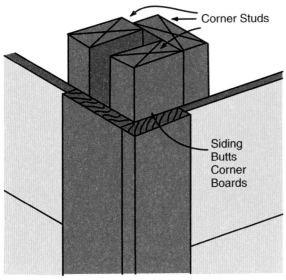

Corner Studs

Siding Butts Corner Boards

Figure 35C - Inset Corner Boards

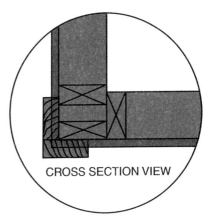

CROSS SECTION VIEW

Window and Door Details

Study the typical window and door details shown in Figures 36A through 36D for examples of door and window framing construction. Because of the great variety in window manufacturing, it is best to study the window manufacturer's installation details before framing and trimming them. Small sheds can utilize a built on-site door constructed from plywood and 1x trim (see Figure 36B). Other shed designs with greater traffic should use an exterior prehung door complete with threshold and side and head jambs (see Figures 36A and 36C).

Figure 36D illustrates the installation of a metal framed window with nail-on flange. These windows are inexpensive, readily available, and relatively easy to install. Consult the manufacturer's installation instructions for precise step-by-step procedures.

Figure 36A - Service Door Jamb Detail

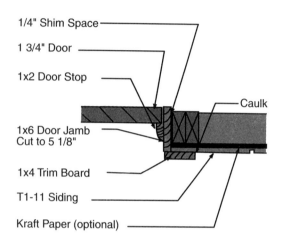

1/4" Shim Space
1 3/4" Door
1x2 Door Stop
Caulk
1x6 Door Jamb Cut to 5 1/8"
1x4 Trim Board
T1-11 Siding
Kraft Paper (optional)

Figure 36B - Built On-Site Barn Door

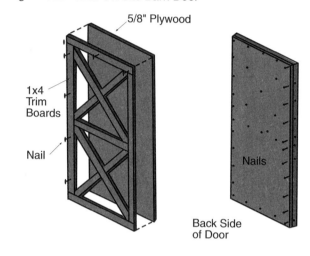

5/8" Plywood
1x4 Trim Boards
Nail
Nails
Back Side of Door

Figure 36C - Service Door Head

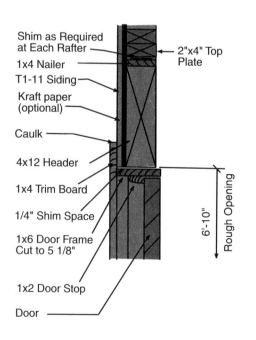

Shim as Required at Each Rafter
1x4 Nailer
T1-11 Siding
Kraft paper (optional)
Caulk
4x12 Header
1x4 Trim Board
1/4" Shim Space
1x6 Door Frame Cut to 5 1/8"
1x2 Door Stop
Door
2"x4" Top Plate
6'-10" Rough Opening

Figure 36D - Metal-Framed Window Installation

When Window is in Place, Staple Building Paper Over Flange

Header

Building Paper

Window Nailing Flange

Roof Shingles

Once the roof sheathing, cornice trim, and fascia boards are in place, the roof shingles can be applied. See the shingle manufacturer's instructions on the bundle. Shingles chosen to harmonize with or match your home are recommended. Square butt shingles are 36" x 12" in size, have three tabs, and are normally laid with 5" exposed to the weather (see Figure 37A).

Start with 15# asphalt felt paper at the bottom edge of the roof. Lap each course 2". After the roofing felt is on, apply a starter course of shingles (shingles turned upside down), lapping over the eave and rake fascia 1/2" to provide a drip edge. Use four nails for each shingle and apply a Boston ridge at top that is made by cutting a shingle into thirds (see Figure 37E). Start at one end of the ridge and fasten with two nails to a shingle leaving a 5" exposure. Cut shingles with a utility knife. Metal drip edges are used in some regions.

For a simple-to-install shed roof, use panel roofing (see Figure 37B). Be sure to overhang the eave by at least 2" and install a ridge cap. You can insert one or two translucent fiberglass roof panels between the solid metal roof panels to provide for natural lighting.

Figure 37A - Shingle Plan

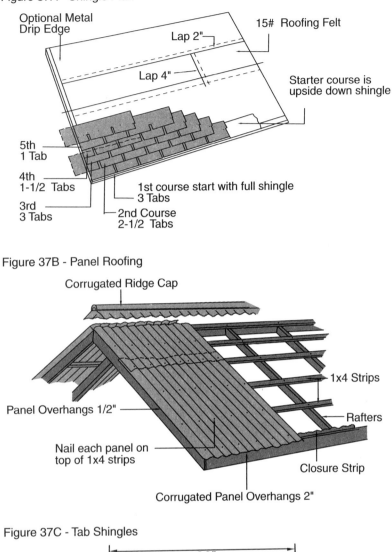

Figure 37B - Panel Roofing

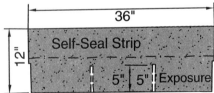

Figure 37C - Tab Shingles

Tab shingles are always applied so that a full tab is centered over a slot below. If length of roof requires a narrow piece to finish first course, start the second row with piece of same width. Continue alternating narrow pieces in each succeeding row.

Figure 37D - Shingle Ridge Detail

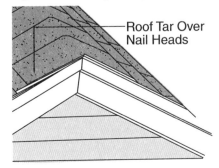

Figure 37E - Cutting A Shingle

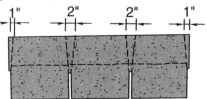

To cut a shingle, score a line with your utility knife, then bend and snap off the piece. Make 3 hip or ridge shingles from one shingle.

Installing Electrical Wiring

Depending on how you are going to utilize your shed, you might want to install electrical wiring (see Figure 38). Two steps are almost mandatory if you plan to supply your shed with electrical service and want to do the job yourself:

1. First check with your local building department and determine the code standards for your area. They will advise you regarding permit and inspection requirements. They will also advise you whether or not there are any requirements for using a professional electrician during wiring.

2. Consult with your local power company. They will inform you if you need a separate electrical service for your shed. If you plan on running off existing home service, they will tell you if your home service can carry the additional load.

If you are allowed to use a branch circuit from your main panel, install an additional Ground Fault Circuit Interrupter (GFCI) type circuit breaker in your main circuit box and then use buried cable (Type UF cable for underground burial) to supply your shed. Be certain that you bury the cable in an area that will not be disturbed by digging or other activity. Certain municipalities might not allow buried cable and will require a separate service installation.

You should install a main disconnect box for electrical service inside your shed. Be sure not to exceed the total amperage rating of the box in your branch circuits. Inside the shed, you can wire lighting and receptacles using either romex (Type NM cable) or metal sheathed cable (Type BX cable) depending upon your local code requirements. If you are wiring a moist area such as a greenhouse or cabana, use Type NMC cable or Type UM for extra protection against moisture. Also install GFCI receptacles in areas with excessive moisture. Consult your local building department for GFCI requirements and regulations.

Figure 38 - Electrical Wiring Options

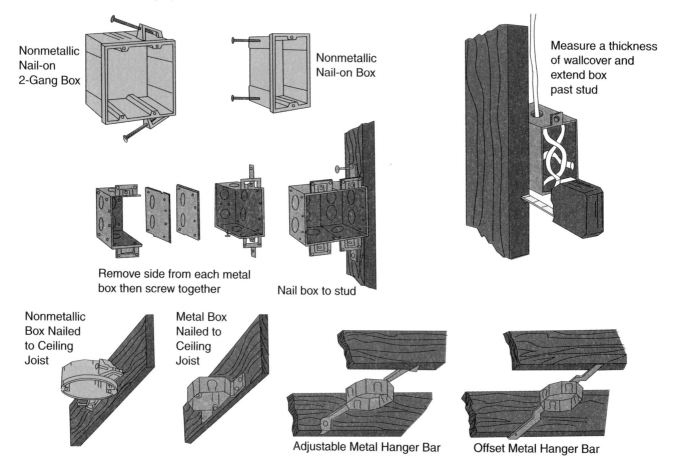

Nonmetallic Nail-on 2-Gang Box

Nonmetallic Nail-on Box

Measure a thickness of wallcover and extend box past stud

Remove side from each metal box then screw together

Nail box to stud

Nonmetallic Box Nailed to Ceiling Joist

Metal Box Nailed to Ceiling Joist

Adjustable Metal Hanger Bar

Offset Metal Hanger Bar

Finishing the Inside of Your Shed

You can either finish the interior of your shed with drywall or leave the wall studs exposed and use blocking to build shelving between the studs. Most storage builders will want to take advantage of the extra storage space afforded by the open wall sections. Use your imagination to create additional storage space by nailing or screwing 1x2 cleats to the studs and then installing extended horizontal shelving over the cleats.

If you elect to install 4'x8' drywall panels (also known as wallboard) in your shed, study the illustrations below for suggestions on nailing or gluing drywall to wall studs.

A variety of fasteners are available for wallboard. Consult your local home center or building material supplier for suggestions. After you have installed the panels, you can tape and fill the joints with joint compound or simply cover the joints with tape if the final appearance is not a major concern.

Figure 39 - Nailing Wallboard

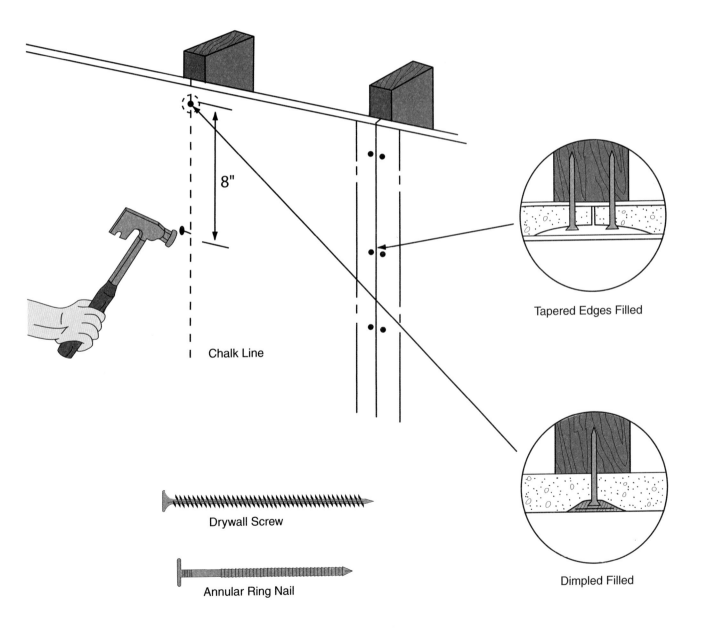

8"

Chalk Line

Drywall Screw

Annular Ring Nail

Tapered Edges Filled

Dimpled Filled

Adding a Ramp to Your Shed

An entry ramp makes life easier for you and your shed. Instead of lugging heavy garden tools such as mowers or snow removal machines up and down from ground level to shed level, use a ramp built from solid 2x material to improve accessibility. If your ramp will be over 3 feet in width, add an additional 2x vertical support to the center of the ramp. Nail the ramp decking to the ramp supports with 12d hot-dipped galvanized nails or use 3" decking screws.

Figure 40A - Design A

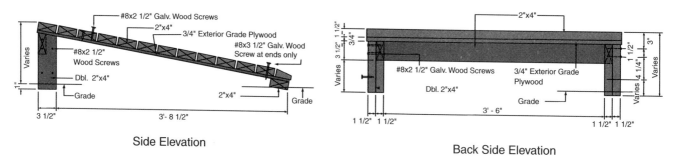

Side Elevation

Back Side Elevation

Figure 40B - Design B

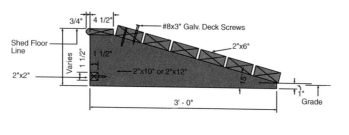

Side Elevation

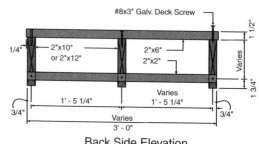

Back Side Elevation

Scale: ¼" = 1'-0" per square

Glossary

Anchor Bolt - A metal connector device used to connect a wood mudsill to a concrete wall or slab.

Batterboards - Scrap lumber nailed horizontally to stakes driven near each corner of the foundation excavation. Stretch nylon strings between batterboards to transfer reference points and to measure elevation.

Beam - Beams are horizontal structural members that are supported by vertical posts. Beams are typically constructed from 2 or more 2-bys, 4-by material, or engineered lumber.

Bottom Plate - In stud wall framing, the bottom horizontal member of the wall. Also known as the soleplate.

Bridging - Wood or metal cross pieces fastened between floor joists to provide structural strength.

Cantilever - Refers to the end portion of a joist that extends beyond the beam.

Casing - Molding around door and window openings.

Codes - Regulations implemented by your local building department which control the design and construction of buildings and other structures. Consult your local building department for applicable codes before you begin your construction project.

Collar Beam - A connecting member used between rafters to strengthen the roof structure.

Cornice - The structure created at the eave overhang which typically consists of fascia board, soffit, and moldings.

Cripple Studs - Short studs that strengthen window and door openings or the gable end of a roof. Also known as jack studs.

Defect - Any defect in lumber whether a result of a manufacturing imperfection or an irregularity in the timber from which the lumber was cut. Some defects are only blemishes while others can reduce strength and durability. Grading rules establish the extent and severity of wood defects.

Drip Edge - Angled metal or wood located on the outer edge of the roof. Drip edge prevents water penetration.

Drywall - A gypsum panel used to finish interior walls. Also known as plasterboard or sheet rock.

Eave - The roof overhang projecting beyond the exterior wall.

Edge - The narrowest side of a piece of lumber which is perpendicular to both the face and the end.

Elevation - Drawing of a structure as it will appear from the front, rear, left and right sides.

Engineered Lumber - Refers to beams or rafters constructed from wood fiber and glue such as glu-lams, micro-lams, or wood I-beams. Often superior in strength and durability to dimensional lumber.

Face - The widest side of a piece of lumber which is perpendicular to both the edge and the end.

Fascia - Trim used along the eave or gable end.

Finish - Any protective coating applied to your structure to protect against weathering. Finishes are available as stains, paints, or preservatives.

Flakeboard - A panel material made from compressed wood chips bonded with resin. Also known as oriented strand board (OSB) or chipboard.

Flashing - Metal material used on the roof and eaves to prevent moisture penetration.

Fly Rafters - Rafters at the gable end which "fly" unsupported by the tie plate. Also known as rack, barge, or verge rafters.

Footing - Concrete footings help to anchor your foundation or piers in the surrounding soil and distribute weight over a larger surface area. In climates where the soil freezes, a generous footing protects against soil heaves and structural slippage.

Frieze - A horizontal framing member that connects the siding with the soffit.

Frost Line - Measure of the maximum penetration of frost in the soil in a given geographic location. Depth of frost penetration varies with climate conditions.

Furring - Narrow strips of wood attached to walls or other surfaces that serve as a fastening base for drywall.

Gable - The triangular end of the roof structure formed by the roof framing.

Galvanized Nails - Hot-dipped galvanized nails (HDG) are dipped in zinc and will not rust.

Girder - Same as beam.

Grade Stamp - A stamp imprinted on dimensional lumber which identifies wood species, grade, texture, moisture content, and usage. Grade descriptions such as select, finish, and common signify limiting characteristics that may occur in lumber in each grade. The stamp indicates a uniform measurement of performance that permits lumber of a given grade to be used for the same purpose, regardless of the manufacturer.

Grading - The process of excavating, leveling, and compacting the soil or gravel beneath your foundation to its desired finish level. Proper grading avoids drainage problems.

Grain - Lumber shows either a flat or vertical grain depending on how it was cut from the log. To minimize warping along the face of decking (known as cupping) and raising of the grain, you should place flat grain decking with the bark side up or facing out.

Header - A horizontal load-bearing support member over an opening in the wall such as window or door openings.

Heartwood - Core of the log that resists decay.

Hip Rafter - A short rafter that forms the hip of a roof and runs from the corner of a wall to the ridge board. Usually set at a 45-degree angle to the walls.

Jack Rafter - A short rafter that runs from the ridge board to a hip or valley rafter or from the hip rafter to the tie plate.

Joist - Lumber which is set on edge and supports a floor, decking, or ceiling. Joists in turn are supported by beams and posts.

Joist Hanger - A metal connector available in many sizes and styles that attaches to a ledge or rim joist and makes a secure butt joint between ledger and joist.

Lag Screw - Heavy-duty fastener with hexagonal bolt head that provides extra fastening power for critical structural connections. Use galvanized lag screws to prevent rust.

Ledger - A horizontal support member to which joists or other support members are attached.

Let-in Brace - Usually a 1x4 corner brace in a wall section that runs diagonally from the bottom to top plate.

Glossary

Look-out - Blocking which extends from an inner common rafter to the fly rafters at the gable ends.

Metal Connectors - Used to augment or replace nails as fasteners, metal connectors are critical for lasting and sturdy garage construction.

Moisture Content - Moisture content of wood is the weight of water in wood expressed as a percentage of the weight of wood from which all water has been removed. The drier the lumber the less the lumber will shrink and warp. Surfaced lumber with a moisture content of 19% or less is known as dry lumber and is typically grade stamped as "S-DRY." Moisture content over 19% results in a "S-GRN" stamp to indicate surfaced green.

Mudsill - The part of the wall framing that contacts the foundation. Should be pressure-treated to resist moisture and decay. Also known as the sill plate.

Outrigger - An extension of a rafter at the eave used to form a cornice or overhang on a roof.

Pea Gravel - Approximately 1/4" round gravel material used in a 4"-6" layer to cover the soil under your concrete slab.

Perpendicular - At a 90 degree or right angle.

Pilot Hole - A slightly undersized hole drilled in lumber which prevents splitting of the wood when nailed.

Pitch - A measurement of roof slope. Expressed as the ratio of the total rise divided by the span.

Plumb - Absolutely vertical. Determined with either a plumb bob or spirit level.

Post - A vertical support member which bears the weight of the joists and beams. Typically posts are at least 4x4 lumber.

Pressure-treated - Refers to the process of forcing preservative compounds into the fiber of the wood. Handle pressure-treated lumber with caution and do not inhale or burn its sawdust. Certain types of pressure-treated lumber are suitable for ground contact use while others must be used above ground. While more expensive than untreated lumber, pressure-treated wood resists decay and is recommended where naturally decay-resistant species like cedar or redwood are unavailable or too costly.

Purlin - A horizontal member of the roof framing that supports rafters or spans between trusses.

Rafter - A roof framing member that extends from the top plate to the ridge board and supports the roof sheeting and roofing material.

Rake - The inclined end area of a gable roof.

Redwood - Decay-resistant and stable wood for exterior use. Heartwood grades provide the greatest decay resistance.

Reinforcing Bar - A steel rod which provides internal reinforcement for concrete piers and foundations. Also known as rebar.

Ridge Board - A 1x or typically 2x member on edge at the roof's peak to which the rafters are connected.

Right Triangle, 6-8-10 or 3-4-5 - A means of ensuring squareness when you lay out your foundations. Mark a vertical line at exactly 8'-0" from the angle you want to square. Then mark a horizontal line at exactly 6'-0" from the crossing vertical line. Measure the distance diagonally between both the 6'-0" and 8'-0" marks and when the distance measures 10'-0" exactly you have squared a 90 degree angle between lines.

Rise - In roof construction the vertical distance the ridge rises above the top plate at the center of the span.

Rough Sill - The lowest framing member of a door or window opening.

Scale - A system of representation in plan drawing where small dimensions represent an equivalent large dimension. Most construction plans are said to be scaled down. Scale is expressed as an equation such as 1/4"=1'-0".

Screed - A straight piece of lumber used to level wet concrete or the gravel.

Sheathing - Exterior sheet (typically 4'x8') material fastened to the rafter or exterior stud walls.

Slope - A measurement of inclination and is expressed as a percentage of units of vertical rise per units of horizontal distance.

Soffit - The underside of the roof overhang. Soffits can either be closed or open (thus exposing the roof rafters).

Span - The distance between two opposing walls as measured from the outside of the top plates or the distance between two beam supports which is measured from center to center.

Spirit Level - A sealed cylinder with a transparent tube nearly filled with liquid forming a bubble used to indicate true vertical and horizontal alignment when the bubble is centered in the length of the tube.

String Level - A spirit level mounted in a frame with prongs at either end for hanging on a string. Determines level across string lines.

Stud - The vertical framing member of a wall.

T1-11 Siding - Exterior siding material with vertical grooves usually 8" on center.

Tie Plate - The framing member nailed to the top plates in order to connect and align wall sections. Also known as the cap plate or second top plate.

Toenail - To drive a nail at an angle. When you toenail a post to a beam for example, drive the nail so that one-half the nail is in each member.

Top Plate - The horizontal top part of the wall framing perpendicular to the wall studs.

Tongue and Groove - Refers to the milling of lumber so that adjacent parts interlock for added strength and durability.

Trimmer Stud - The stud adjacent to window or door opening studs which strengthens the opening and bears the weight of the window or door headers. Also known as a jack stud.

Truss - A triangular prefabricated unit for supporting a roof load over a span. Trusses are relatively lightweight and can offer an easier method of roof construction for the novice.

Valley Rafter - A rafter running from a tie plate at the corner of a wall along the roof valley and up to the ridge.

Ready to Start Some Serious Planning?

Now that you have read this do-it-yourself manual, you're ready to start serious planning. As you can see, there are many details to consider, and they all tie together for successful completion of your shed project.

If the procedures appear at first confusing, reread the information outlined in this book several times before deciding which phases of construction you want to handle yourself and which might require professional assistance.

Because drawing up your own plan from scratch can be time consuming and difficult for the inexperienced builder, you might want to make planning and cost estimating easier by selecting a design from those shown in this book.

If blueprints with lumber lists are not immediately available from your building material dealer, you can order them by using the order form in the back of this book. If after reviewing the blueprints you still have questions, talk them over with your lumber dealer. Most dealers are familiar with construction and will be glad to help you.

The following pages include an assortment of shed plans and shed-related plans. Remember that construction blueprints can be obtained from your dealer or by using the order form on page 80. All blueprint plans include a complete material list, exterior elevations, sections, details and instructions for the successful completion of your shed project.

Example of a Typical Project Plan Sheet

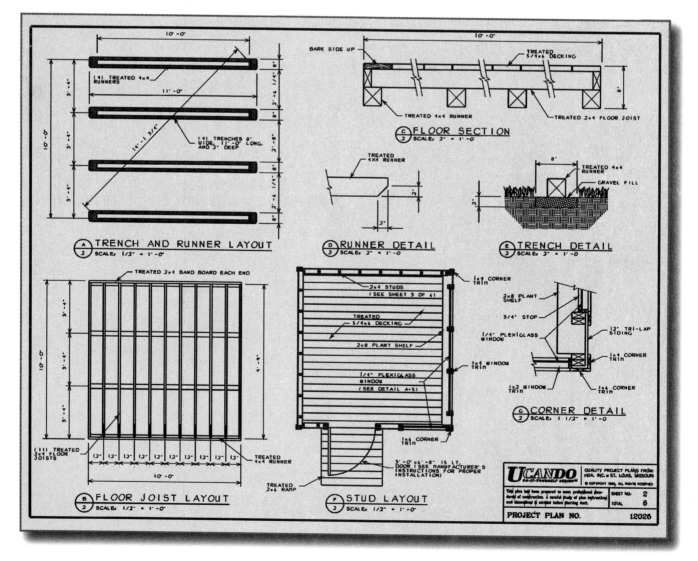

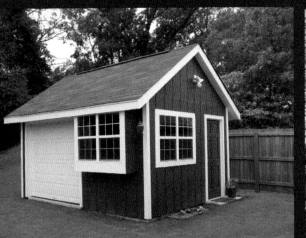

Project Plans

SHEDS, PLAYHOUSES, CABANAS AND MORE

Barn Storage Sheds with Loft

PRICE CODE P7

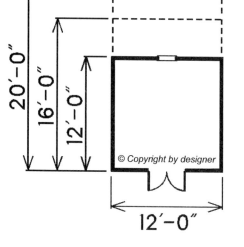

PLAN #SM3-002D-4501

- Three popular sizes -
    12' x 12'   12' x 16'   12' x 20'
- Pier or slab foundation
- Height floor to peak - 12'-10"
- Ceiling height - 7'-4"
- 4' x 6'-8" double-door for easy access
- Complete list of materials
- Step-by-step instructions

Convenience Shed

PRICE CODE P7

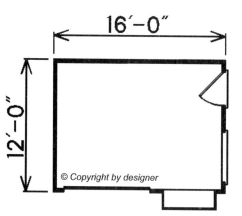

PLAN #SM3-002D-4506

- Size - 16' x 12'
- Slab foundation
- Height floor to peak - 12'- 4 1/2"
- Ceiling height - 8'
- 8' x 7' overhead door
- Ideal for lawn equipment or small boat storage
- Oversized windows brighten interior
- Complete list of materials
- Step-by-step instructions

Garden Sheds with Clerestory

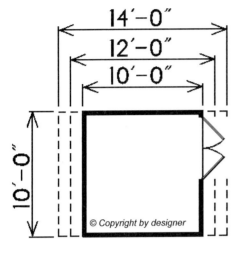

PLAN #SM3-002D-4515

- Three popular sizes -
  - 10' x 10'   12' x 10'   14' x 10'
- Wood floor on 4x6 runners
- Height floor to peak - 10'-11"
- Rear wall height - 7'-3"
- 5' x 6'-9" double-door for easy access
- Clerestory windows for added light
- Complete list of materials
- Step-by-step instructions

Yard Barn with Loft Storage

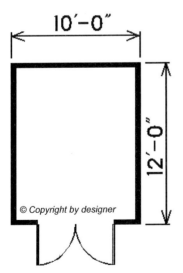

PLAN #SM3-002D-4520

- Size - 10' x 12'
- Wood floor on 4x4 runners
- Height floor to peak - 10'-7"
- Ceiling height - 6'-11"
- 6' x 6'-2" double-door for easy access
- Loft provides additional storage area
- Attractive styling is suitable for any yard
- Complete list of materials
- Step-by-step instructions

Children's Playhouse

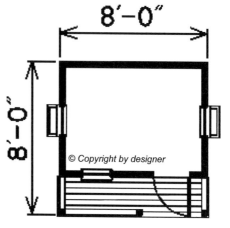

8'-0"

8'-0"

© Copyright by designer

PLAN #SM3-002D-4505

- Size - 8' x 8'
- Wood floor on 4x4 runners
- Height floor to peak - 9'-2"
- Ceiling height - 6'-1"
- 2' deep porch
- Attractive window boxes
- Includes operable windows
- Complete list of materials
- Step-by-step instructions

Screened Shelter with Kitchen

17'-0"

22'-0"

Bath

Stor.

Kit.

REF.

Vaulted ceiling

Screened Patio

© Copyright by designer

Opt. Hot Tub

Porch

PLAN #SM3-009D-7528

- Size - 17' x 22'
- Slab foundation
- Building height - 17'
- Ceiling heights -
    Kitchen and bath - 9'   Patio area - 13'
- Roof pitch - 10/12
- The ideal shelter for a hot tub or lounging furniture
- Features a vaulted ceiling, fireplace, kitchen and half bath
- Complete list of materials

PRICE CODE P8

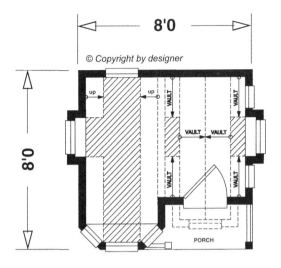

8'0

8'0

© Copyright by designer

PORCH

Whipplewood Cottage

PLAN #SM3-063D-4511

- Size - 8' x 8'
- Pier or slab foundation
- Building height - 8'
- Ceiling height - 6'
- Roof pitch - 4/12, 10/12
- Victorian details add flair to this playhouse
- Complete list of materials
- Plans are printed on 8 1/2" x 11" pages

PRICE CODE P12

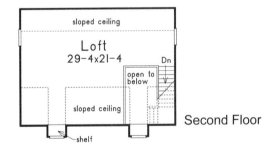

sloped ceiling

Loft
29-4x21-4   Dn

open to below

sloped ceiling

shelf

Second Floor

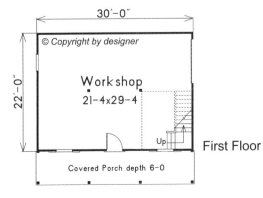

30'-0"

© Copyright by designer

22'-0"

Workshop
21-4x29-4

Up

First Floor

Covered Porch depth 6-0

Workshop with Loft

PLAN #SM3-005D-7500

- Size - 30' x 22'
- Slab foundation
- Building height - 20'-6"
- Ceiling height - 8'
- 8' x 7' overhead door
- Roof pitch - 6/12, 8/12
- Open floor plan has ample workspace and additional storage with loft above
- Complete list of materials

Cabana with Porch and Bar

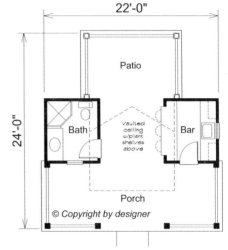

22'-0"

24'-0"

Patio

Bath

Vaulted ceiling w/plant shelves above

Bar

Porch

© Copyright by designer

PLAN #SM3-009D-7524

- Size - 22' x 24'
- Slab foundation
- Building height - 16'-6"
- Ceiling heights -
    Bar and bath - 8'   Vaulted patio area - 13'-6"
- Roof pitch - 4.5/12, 8/12
- A bath and open walk-up/walk-in bar featuring a designated wall for a plasma TV is conveniently located for the porch and patio
- Complete list of materials

Large Poolside Structure

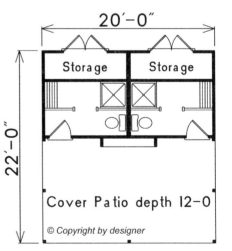

20'-0"

22'-0"

Storage

Storage

Cover Patio depth 12-0

© Copyright by designer

PLAN #SM3-002D-7523

- Size - 20' x 22'
- Slab foundation
- Building height - 13'-5"
- Ceiling height - 8'
- Roof pitch - 6/12
- Two dressing areas both with shower and toilet
- Covered area is ideal for a snack/drink bar
- Complete list of materials
- Step-by-step instructions

Pavilion with Bar, Bath and Sauna

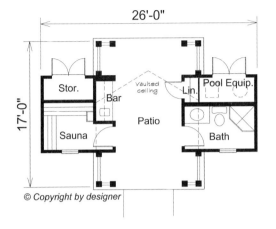

© Copyright by designer

26'-0"

17'-0"

Stor. / Bar / Sauna / Patio / Vaulted ceiling / Lin. / Pool Equip. / Bath

PLAN #SM3-009D-7527

- Size - 26' x 17'
- Slab foundation
- Building height - 13'
- Ceiling heights -
    Bath and sauna - 8'
    Patio with vaulted ceiling - 10'-8"
- Roof pitch - 8/12
- A walk-up bar, sauna, bath and two storage rooms are convenient to the covered patio
- Complete list of materials

Pool Cabana with Bar

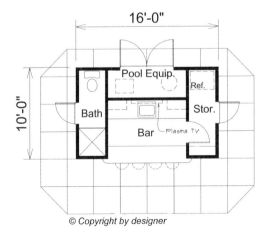

© Copyright by designer

16'-0"

10'-0"

Pool Equip. / Ref. / Bath / Stor. / Bar / Plasma TV

PLAN #SM3-009D-7525

- Size - 16' x 10'
- Slab foundation
- Building height - 11'
- Ceiling height - 8'
- Roof pitch - 5/12
- Features a walk-in bar, cabinetry for storage and a designated wall for a plasma TV
- Features a bath, storage room, and pool equipment room
- Complete list of materials

Deluxe Cabana

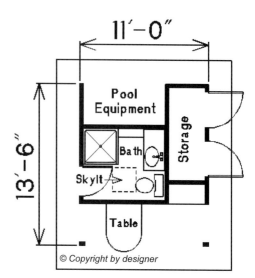

11'-0"

13'-6"

Pool Equipment

Bath

Storage

Skylt

Table

© Copyright by designer

PLAN #SM3-002D-4518

- Size - 11' x 13'-6"
- Slab foundation
- Height floor to peak - 11'-7"
- Ceiling height - 8'
- Unique roof design with skylight
- Convenient dressing room and servicing area
- Perfect storage for poolside furniture and equipment
- Complete list of materials
- Step-by-step instructions

Storage Shed

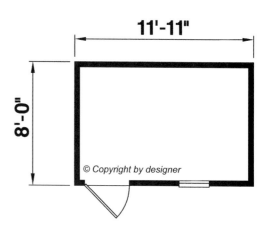

11'-11"

8'-0"

© Copyright by designer

PLAN #SM3-063D-4514

- Size - 11'-11" x 8'
- Pier or slab foundation
- Building height - 8'-6"
- Ceiling height - 6'-6"
- Roof pitch - 4/12
- Complements traditional home exterior
- Could easily be converted to a children's playhouse
- Complete list of materials
- Plans are printed on 8 1/2" x 11" pages

PRICE CODE P6

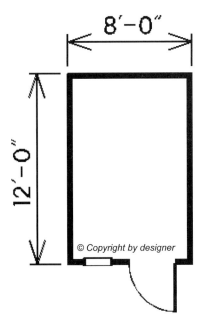

© Copyright by designer

PLAN #SM3-002D-4512

- Size - 8' x 12'
- Pier or slab foundation
- Height floor to peak - 10'-6"
- Ceiling height - 7'
- 3' x 6' door
- Ideal playhouse in summer
- Storage shed in the off-season
- Complete list of materials
- Step-by-step instructions

PRICE CODE P7

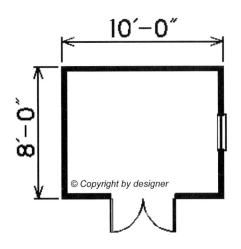

© Copyright by designer

Salt Box Storage Shed

PLAN #SM3-002D-4519

- Size - 10' x 8'
- Wood floor on 4x4 runners
- Height floor to peak - 9'-6"
- Front wall height - 8'
- 4' x 6'-8" double-door for easy access
- Window adds light to interior
- Complete list of materials
- Step-by-step instructions

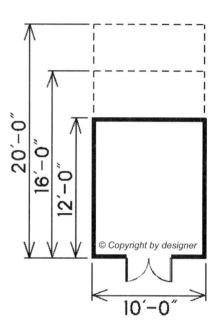

© Copyright by designer

PLAN #SM3-002D-4504

- Three popular sizes -
    10' x 12'   10' x 16'   10' x 20'
- Wood floor on 4x4 runners
- Height floor to peak - 8'-8 1/2"
- Ceiling height - 7'
- 4' x 6'-4" double-door for easy access
- Complete list of materials
- Step-by-step instructions

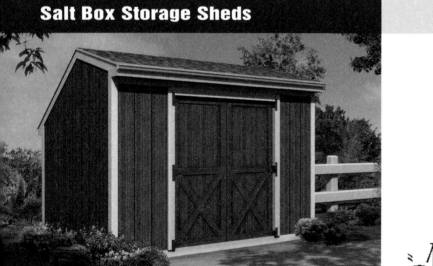

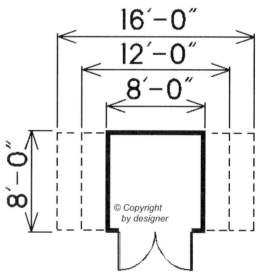

© Copyright by designer

PLAN #SM3-002D-4500

- Three popular sizes -
    8' x 8   12' x 8"   16' x 8'
- Wood floor on gravel base or slab foundation
- Height floor to peak - 8'-2"
- Front wall height - 7'
- 6' x 6'-5" double-door for easy access
- Complete list of materials
- Step-by-step instructions

Gable Storage Sheds

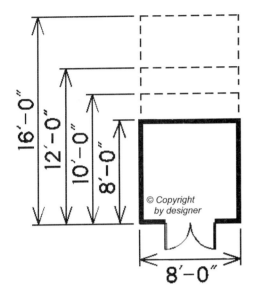

© Copyright
by designer

16'-0"
12'-0"
10'-0"
8'-0"

8'-0"

PLAN #SM3-002D-4503

- Four popular sizes -
    - 8' x 8'   8' x 12'
    - 8' x 10'   8' x 16'
- Wood floor on 4x4 runners
- Height floor to peak - 8'-4 1/2"
- Ceiling height - 6'-9 1/2"
- 4' x 6'-5" double-door for easy access
- Economical and easy to build shed
- Complete list of materials
- Step-by-step instructions

Barn Storage Sheds

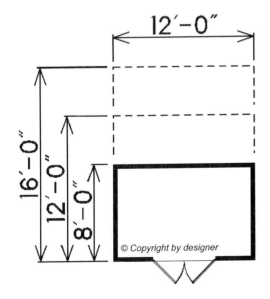

12'-0"

16'-0"
12'-0"
8'-0"

© Copyright by designer

PLAN #SM3-002D-4508

- Three popular sizes -
    - 12' x 8'   12' x 12'   12' x 16'
- Pier or slab foundation
- Height floor to peak - 9'-10"
- Ceiling height - 7'-10"
- 5'-6" x 6'-8" double-door for easy access
- Complete list of materials
- Step-by-step instructions

Garden Shed with Skylights

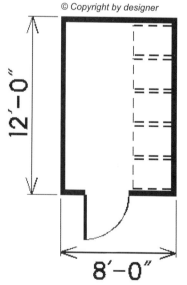

© Copyright by designer

12'-0"

10'-0"

PLAN #SM3-002D-4507

- Size - 10' x 12'
- Wood floor on gravel base
- Height floor to peak - 9'-9"
- Rear wall height - 7'-1 1/2"
- Skylight windows provide optimal plant growth
- Ample room for tool and lawn equipment storage
- Complete list of materials
- Step-by-step instructions

Greenhouse

© Copyright by designer

12'-0"

8'-0"

PLAN #SM3-002D-4513

- Size - 8' x 12'
- Gravel floor with concrete foundation wall
- Height foundation to peak - 8'-3"
- Rear wall height - 7'-11"
- An attractive addition to any yard
- Convenient storage for lawn and garden tools
- Complete list of materials
- Step-by-step instructions

PRICE CODE P7

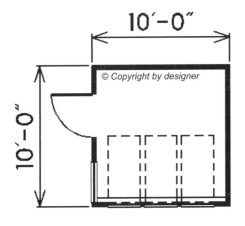

Garden Shed

PLAN #SM3-002D-4523

- Size - 10' x 10'
- Wood floor on 4x4 runners
- Height floor to peak - 11'-3 1/2"
- Left wall height - 8'
- Wonderful complement to any backyard
- Perfect space for lawn equipment or plants and flowers
- Plenty of windows for gardening year-round
- Complete list of materials
- Step-by-step instructions

PRICE CODE P7

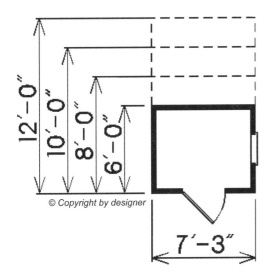

Mini-Barn Storage Sheds

PLAN #SM3-002D-4510

- Four popular sizes -
  - 7'-3" x 6'   7'-3" x 10'
  - 7'-3" x 8'   7'-3" x 12'
- Wood floor on 4x6 runners or slab foundation
- Height floor to peak - 9'
- Ceiling height - 7'-4"
- 3' x 6'-8" door
- Complete list of materials
- Step-by-step instructions

Shed with Playhouse Loft

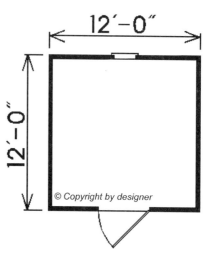

12´-0˝

12´-0˝

© Copyright by designer

PLAN #SM3-002D-4514

- Size - 12' x 12' with 2'-8" deep balcony
- Pier or slab foundation
- Height floor to peak - 14'-1"
- Ceiling height - 7'-4"
- 4' x 6'-10" door
- Loft above can be used as playhouse for children
- Loft features ladder for easy access
- Complete list of materials
- Step-by-step instructions

Yard Barns

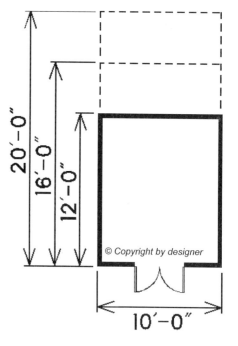

20´-0˝

16´-0˝

12´-0˝

© Copyright by designer

10´-0˝

PLAN #SM3-002D-4502

- Three popular sizes -
  - 10' x 12'   10' x 20'
  - 10' x 16'
- Wood floor on 4x4 runners
- Height floor to peak - 8'-4 1/2"
- Ceiling height - 6'-4"
- 4' x 6'-4" double-door for easy access
- Complete list of materials
- Step-by-step instructions

Barn Shed with Overhead Door

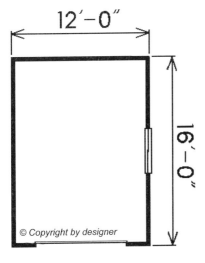

© Copyright by designer

PLAN #SM3-002D-4521

- Size - 12' x 16'
- Slab foundation
- Height floor to peak - 12'-5"
- Ceiling height - 8'
- 8' x 7' overhead door for easy entry with large equipment
- Side windows add light to interior
- Complete list of materials
- Step-by-step instructions

Mini Barns

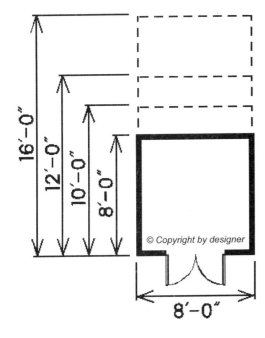

© Copyright by designer

PLAN #SM3-002D-4524

- Four popular sizes -
  - 8' x 8'   8' x 12'
  - 8' x 10'   8' x 16'
- Wood floor on 4x4 runners
- Height floor to peak - 7'-6"
- Ceiling height - 6'
- 4' x 6' double-door for easy access
- Complete list of materials
- Step-by-step instructions

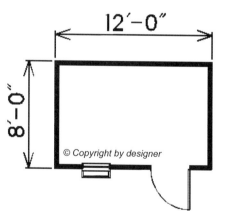

PLAN #SM3-002D-4516

- Size - 10' x 6'
- Wood floor on gravel base
- Height floor to peak - 9'-7"
- Ceiling height - 6'-7"
- 5' x 6'-9" double-door for easy access
- Log storage area - 2'-6" x 6'
- Complete list of materials
- Step-by-step instructions

10'-0"

6'-0"

© Copyright by designer

Gable Storage Shed / Playhouse

PRICE CODE P6

PLAN #SM3-002D-4522

- Size - 12' x 8'
- Wood floor on 4x4 runners
- Height floor to peak - 10'-5"
- Ceiling height - 8'
- 3' x 6'-8" Dutch door
- Perfect for storage or playhouse for children
- Shutters and window box create a charming facade
- Complete list of materials
- Step-by-step instructions

12'-0"

8'-0"

© Copyright by designer

Gable Shed with Cupola

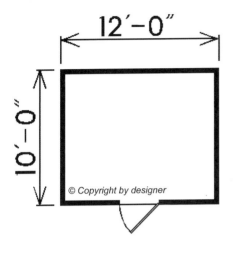

PLAN #SM3-002D-4511

- Size - 12' x 10'
- Pier or slab foundation
- Height floor to peak - 9'-8"
- Ceiling height - 7'-4"
- 3' x 6'-8" door
- Made of cedar plywood with battens
- Complete list of materials
- Step-by-step instructions

Gable Storage Sheds

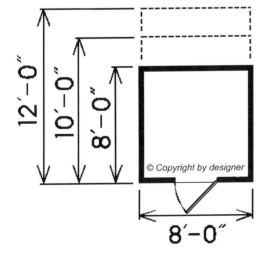

PLAN #SM3-002D-4509

- Three popular sizes -
  8' x 8'   8' x 10'   8' x 12'
- Wood floor on concrete footings
- Height floor to peak - 9'-1"
- Wall height - 6'-7"
- Circle-top window adds interest and light
- Complete list of materials
- Step-by-step instructions

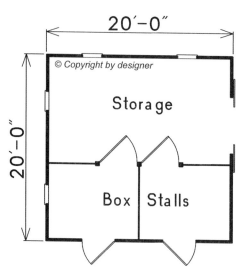

PLAN #SM3-002D-7521

- Size - 20' x 20'
- Partial slab foundation
- Building height - 12'-8"
- Ceiling height - 8'
- 6' x 7' sliding side door into storage area
- Roof pitch - 5/12
- Compact, yet extra storage for feed
- Complete list of materials

Pole Building

PRICE CODE P12

PLAN #SM3-002D-7506

- Size - 32' x 40'
- Dirt floor
- Building height - 16'
- Ceiling height - 10'
- 10' x 8' sliding door
- Roof pitch - 4/12
- Complete list of materials
- Step-by-step instructions

PRICE CODE P12

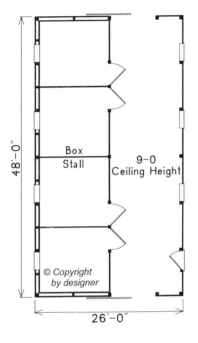

PLAN #SM3-002D-7511

- Size - 26' x 48'
- Compacted clay floor in stalls, concrete slab floor
- Building height - 22'
- Ceiling height - 9'   Loft ceiling height - 11'
- Two 8' x 8' sliding doors and one
  5' x 7' sliding door at loft
- Roof pitch - 6/12
- Loft designed for 75 p.s.f. live load
- Complete list of materials
- Step-by-step instructions

PRICE CODE P11

Pole Building - Equipment Shed

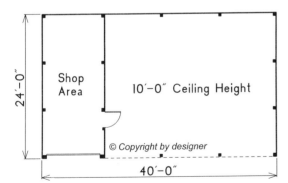

PLAN #SM3-002D-7505

- Size - 40' x 24'
- Concrete slab in shop area
- Building height - 14'-4"
- Ceiling height - 10'
- 9' x 8' overhead door
- Roof pitch - 4/12
- This design can be lengthened by adding 10' bays
- Complete list of materials
- Step-by-step instructions

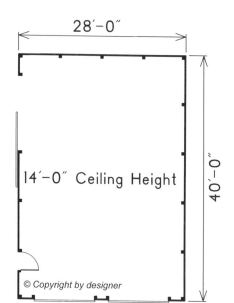

28'-0"

40'-0"

14'-0" Ceiling Height

© Copyright by designer

PLAN #SM3-002D-7500

- Size - 28' x 40'
- Dirt floor
- Building height - 19'-6"
- Ceiling height - 14'
- Two 10' x 10' overhead doors and one 12' x 12' sliding door
- Roof pitch - 4/12
- Designed for easy maintenance
- Complete list of materials
- Step-by-step instructions

Pole Buildings

PRICE CODE P12

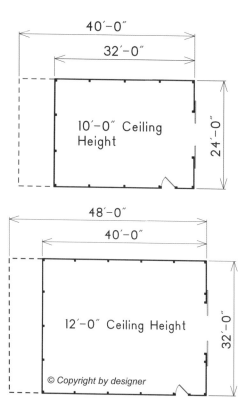

40'-0"

32'-0"

10'-0" Ceiling Height

24'-0"

48'-0"

40'-0"

12'-0" Ceiling Height

32'-0"

© Copyright by designer

PLAN #SM3-002D-7503

- Four popular sizes -
    24' x 32'   32' x 40'
    24' x 40'   32' x 48'
- Dirt floor
- Building height - 15'-6" with 10' ceiling height
- Building height - 17'-6" with 12' ceiling height
- Two 5' x 10' or two 6' x 12' sliding doors
- Complete list of materials
- Step-by-step instructions

Multi-Purpose Barn

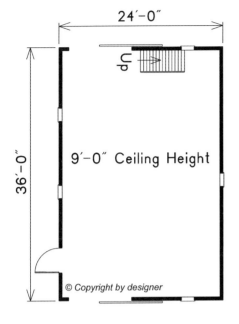

24'-0"

Up

36'-0"

9'-0" Ceiling Height

© Copyright by designer

PLAN #SM3-002D-7501

- Size - 24' x 36'
- Slab or floating slab foundation
- Building height - 23'-8"
- Ceiling height - 9'   Loft ceiling height - 9'-8"
- Two 9' x 9' sliding doors and
  5' x 6' loft double-door
- Roof pitch - 4/12, 12/4
- Loft designed for 100 p.s.f. live load
- Complete list of materials
- Step-by-step instructions

Pole Building - Machine Shed

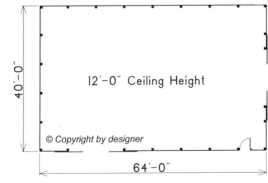

40'-0"

12'-0" Ceiling Height

© Copyright by designer

64'-0"

PLAN #SM3-002D-7507

- Size - 40' x 64'
- Dirt floor
- Building height - 20'
- Ceiling height - 12'
- Two 8' x 10' sliding doors on two sides
  of the building
- Roof pitch - 4/12
- Complete list of materials
- Step-by-step instructions

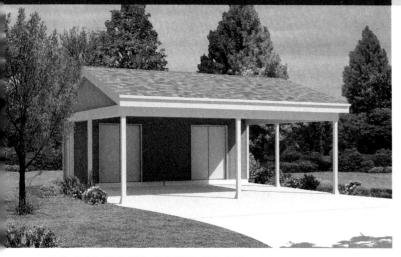

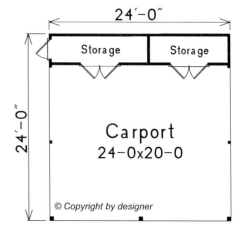

24'-0"

Storage   Storage

24'-0"

Carport
24-0x20-0

© Copyright by designer

PLAN #SM3-002D-6045

- Size - 24' x 24'
- Slab foundation
- Building height - 12'-8"
- Ceiling height - 8'
- Roof pitch - 4/12
- Unique design allows cars to enter from the front or the side of carport
- Deep storage space for long or tall items
- Complete list of materials
- Step-by-step instructions

Workroom with Covered Porch

PRICE CODE P9

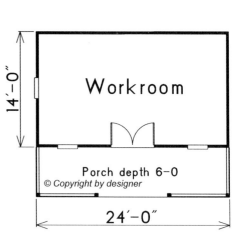

14'-0"

Workroom

Porch depth 6-0
© Copyright by designer

24'-0"

PLAN #SM3-002D-7520

- Size - 24' x 20'
- Slab foundation
- Building height - 13'-6"
- Ceiling height - 8'
- Roof pitch - 6/12
- Easy access through double-door entry
- Interior enhanced by large windows
- Complete list of materials
- Step-by-step instructions

Weekender Cottage

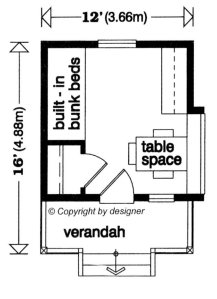

12' (3.66m)

16' (4.88m)

built - in bunk beds

table space

© Copyright by designer

verandah

PLAN #SM3-063D-7500

- Size - 12' x 16'
- Slab foundation
- Building height -14'-6"
- Ceiling height - 10'
- Roof pitch - 5/12, 12/12
- 2" x 6" exterior walls
- Cottage is 144 square feet and could be a home office or guest house
- Multiple built-ins make storage simple
- Complete list of materials

Studio Home Office

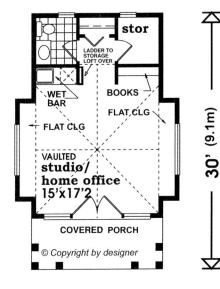

20' (6.1m)

30' (9.1m)

stor

LADDER TO STORAGE LOFT OVER

WET BAR

BOOKS

FLAT CLG

FLAT CLG

VAULTED
studio/ home office
15'x17'2

COVERED PORCH

© Copyright by designer

PLAN #SM3-063D-7501

- Size - 20' x 30'
- Crawl space or slab foundation
- Building height - 19'-6"
- Ceiling height - 9'
- Roof pitch - 12/12
- 2" x 6" exterior walls
- Studio/home office is 432 square feet and brightened by windows
- Complete list of materials

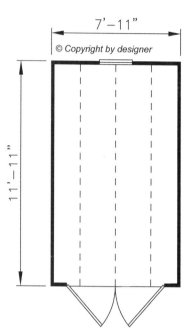

© Copyright by designer

7'-11"

11'-11"

PLAN #SM3-063D-4502

- Size - 7'-11" x 11'-11"
- Pier or slab foundation
- Building height - 8'
- Ceiling height - 6'
- Complete list of materials
- Plans are printed on 8 1/2" x 11" pages

7'-11"

12'-0"

© Copyright by designer

PLAN #SM3-063D-4507

- Size - 7'-11" x 12'
- Pier or slab foundation
- Building height - 9'
- Ceiling height - 6'-6"
- Roof pitch - 4/12
- Barnyard-style door
- Narrow design allows this shed to fit most anywhere
- Complete list of materials
- Plans are printed on 8 1/2" x 11" pages

Garden Shed with Porch

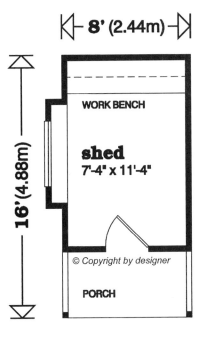

8' (2.44m)

16' (4.88m)

WORK BENCH

shed
7'-4" x 11'-4"

© Copyright by designer

PORCH

PLAN #SM3-063D-4500

- Size - 8' x 16'
- Pier or slab foundation
- Building height -11'
- Ceiling height - 8'
- Roof pitch - 7/12
- Covered front porch
- Handy built-in work bench
- Complete list of materials
- Plans are printed on 8 1/2" x 11" pages

Econo Barn

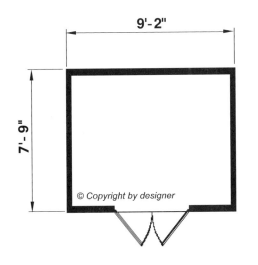

9'-2"

7'-9"

© Copyright by designer

PLAN #SM3-063D-4501

- Size - 9'-2" x 7'-9"
- Slab foundation
- Building height - 8'
- Ceiling height - 4'-9"
- Double-door for easy access
- Complete list of materials
- Plans are printed on 8 1/2" x 11" pages

PLAN #SM3-063D-4509

- Size - 8' x 6'
- Pier foundation or wood floor on concrete blocks
- Building height - 8'-6"
- Ceiling height - 4'-9"
- Roof pitch - 10/12
- Charming covered porch
- Complete list of materials
- Plans are printed on 8 1/2" x 11" pages

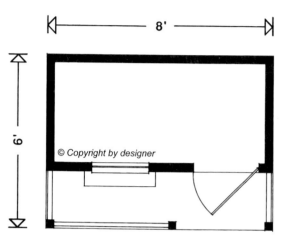

© Copyright by designer

PLAN #SM3-063D-4508

- Size - 6' x 8'
- Pier foundation or wood floor on concrete blocks
- Building height - 8'-6"
- Ceiling height - 4'-8"
- Roof pitch - 10/12
- Charming cottage makes an ideal children's playhouse
- Petite covered porch adds a nice touch
- Complete list of materials
- Plans are printed on 8 1/2" x 11" pages

© Copyright by designer

Craft Cottage

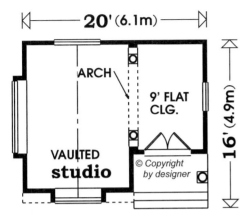

20' (6.1m) — 16' (4.9m)

ARCH

9' FLAT CLG.

VAULTED **studio**

© Copyright by designer

PLAN #SM3-063D-7505

- Size - 20' x 16'
- Crawl space foundation, drawings also include slab foundation
- Building height - 16'-8"
- Ceiling height - 9'
- Roof pitch - 5/12, 12/12
- 2" x 6" exterior walls
- Charming cottage is 288 square feet
- Double French doors access covered porch
- Complete list of materials

Garden Shed with Playhouse

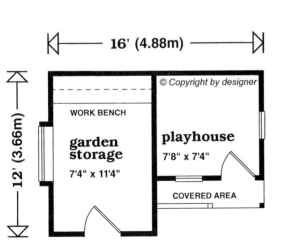

16' (4.88m) — 12' (3.66m)

© Copyright by designer

WORK BENCH

garden storage
7'4" x 11'4"

playhouse
7'8" x 7'4"

COVERED AREA

PLAN #SM3-063D-4510

- Size - 16' x 12'
- Pier or slab foundation
- Building height - 13'
- Ceiling heights - 7', 8'
- Roof pitch - 12/12
- Garden shed with playhouse combines efficiency with fun
- Charming country cottage style
- Complete list of materials
- Plans are printed on 8 1/2" x 11" pages

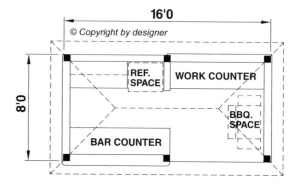

16'0
8'0

REF. SPACE | WORK COUNTER
BBQ. SPACE
BAR COUNTER

© Copyright by designer

PLAN #SM3-063D-4506

- Size - 16' x 8'
- Slab foundation
- Building height - 13'
- Ceiling height - 9'-6"
- Convenient space for outdoor entertaining features barbecue area, refrigerator space and eating and preparation counters
- Complete list of materials
- Plans are printed on 8 1/2" x 11" pages

Rustic Pool Cabana

PRICE CODE P7

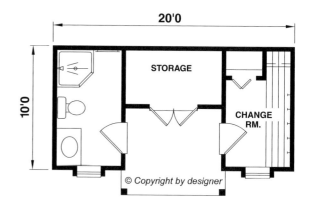

20'0
10'0

STORAGE
CHANGE RM.

© Copyright by designer

PLAN #SM3-063D-4504

- Size - 20' x 10'
- Slab foundation
- Building height - 11'-6"
- Ceiling height - 8'
- Roof pitch - 7/12
- Rustic cabin feel
- Pool cabana includes storage, a bath and a changing room
- Complete list of materials
- Plans are printed on 8 1/2" x 11" pages

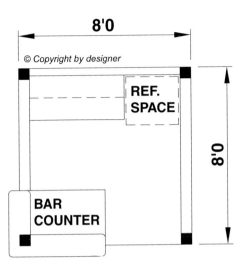

8'0

© Copyright by designer

REF. SPACE

8'0

BAR COUNTER

PLAN #SM3-063D-4505

- Size - 8' x 8'
- Slab foundation
- Building height - 13'
- Ceiling height - 9'-6"
- Summer pavilion is perfect for outdoor entertaining and features built-in shelves, bar counter and space for a refrigerator
- Complete list of materials
- Plans are printed on 8 1/2" x 11" pages

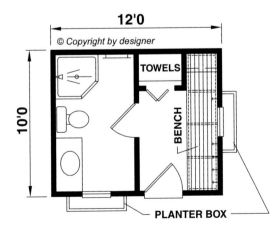

12'0

© Copyright by designer

TOWELS

BENCH

10'0

PLANTER BOX

PLAN #SM3-063D-4503

- Size - 12' x 10'
- Slab foundation
- Building height - 11'-6"
- Ceiling height - 8'
- Roof pitch - 7/12
- Charming cabana is 120 square feet and has a bath, towel storage and dressing area
- Complete list of materials
- Plans are printed on 8 1/2" x 11" pages

PLAN #SM3-063D-4512

- Size - 7'-11" x 8'
- Pier or slab foundation
- Building height - 8'-6"
- Ceiling height - 6'-6"
- Roof pitch - 4/12
- Ample storage space for lawn or garden equipment
- Complete list of materials
- Plans are printed on 8 1/2" x 11" pages

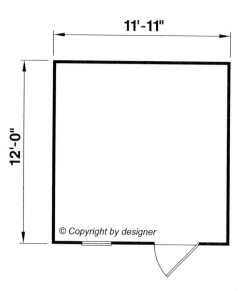

© Copyright by designer

7'-11"

8'-0"

PLAN #SM3-063D-4513

- Size - 11'-11" x 12'
- Pier or slab foundation
- Building height - 9'
- Ceiling height - 6'-6"
- Roof pitch - 4/12
- Easily accommodates large yard equipment
- Shed can easily be converted to a workshop
- Complete list of materials
- Plans are printed on 8 1/2" x 11" pages

11'-11"

12'-0"

© Copyright by designer

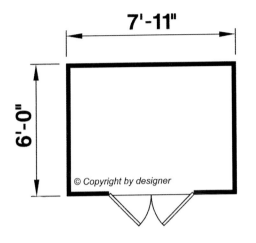

7'-11"

6'-0"

© Copyright by designer

PLAN #SM3-063D-4516

- Size - 7'-11" x 6'
- Pier or slab foundation
- Building height - 8'
- Front wall height - 7'-6"
- Roof pitch - 4/12
- Wide double doors allow for easy storage
- Complete list of materials
- Plans are printed on 8 1/2" x 11" pages

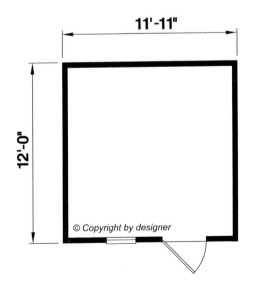

11'-11"

12'-0"

© Copyright by designer

PLAN #SM3-063D-4515

- Size - 11'-11" x 12'
- Pier or slab foundation
- Building height - 9'
- Ceiling height - 6'-6"
- Roof pitch - 4/12
- Interior brightened by front window
- Complete list of materials

Salt Box Storage Shed

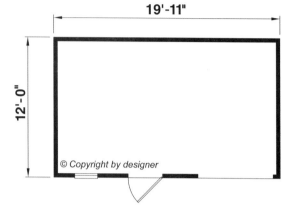

PLAN #SM3-063D-4517

- Size - 19'-11" x 12'
- Pier or slab foundation
- Building height - 9'
- Ceiling height - 6'-6"
- Roof pitch - 4/12
- Complete list of materials
- Plans are printed on 8 1/2" x 11" pages

Yard and Garden Shed

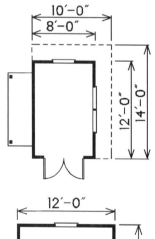

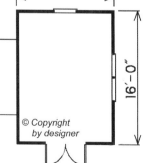

PLAN #SM3-064D-4500

- Three popular sizes
  - 8' x 12'   10' x 14'   12' x 16'
- Wood floor on 4x4 runners or slab foundation
- Height floor to peak - 11'-6"
- Ceiling height - 8'
- 5' x 6'-8" double-door for easy access
- 3' x 9' side storage with overhang
- Complete list of materials
- Step-by-step instructions

PRICE CODE P7

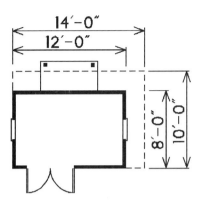

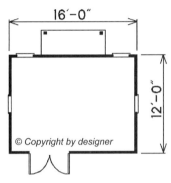

© Copyright by designer

Salt Box Storage Shed

PLAN #SM3-064D-4501

- Three popular sizes-
  - 12' x 8'   14' x 10'   16' x 12'
- Wood floor on 4x4 runners or slab foundation
- Height floor to peak - 12'-6"
- Ceiling height - 8'
- 5' x 6'-8" double-door for easy access
- Complete list of materials
- Step-by-step instructions

PRICE CODE P7

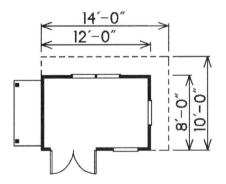

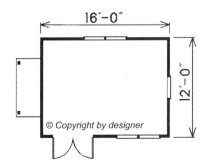

© Copyright by designer

Utility Shed

PLAN #SM3-064D-4502

- Three popular sizes -
  - 12' x 8'   14' x 10'   16' x 12'
- Wood floor on 4x4 runners or slab foundation
- Height floor to peak - 11'-6"
- Ceiling height - 8'
- 5' x 6'-8" double-door for easy access
- Complete list of materials
- Step-by-step instructions

Project Plan Index

Plan #	Price Code	Page	Reproducibles/ PDF Available	Plan#	Price Code	Page	Reproducibles/ PDF Available
SM3-002D-4500	P7	54	X	SM3-002D-7520	P9	66	X
SM3-002D-4501	P7	46	X	SM3-002D-7521	P9	62	X
SM3-002D-4502	P7	58	X	SM3-002D-7523	P9	50	X
SM3-002D-4503	P7	55	X	SM3-005D-7500	P12	49	X
SM3-002D-4504	P7	54	X	SM3-009D-7524	P9	50	X
SM3-002D-4505	P6	48	X	SM3-009D-7525	P8	51	X
SM3-002D-4506	P7	46	X	SM3-009D-7527	P8	51	X
SM3-002D-4507	P7	56	X	SM3-009D-7528	P8	48	X
SM3-002D-4508	P7	55	X	SM3-063D-4500	P7	69	
SM3-002D-4509	P6	61	X	SM3-063D-4501	P7	69	
SM3-002D-4510	P7	57	X	SM3-063D-4502	P7	68	
SM3-002D-4511	P7	61	X	SM3-063D-4503	P7	73	
SM3-002D-4512	P6	53	X	SM3-063D-4504	P7	72	
SM3-002D-4513	P7	56	X	SM3-063D-4505	P6	73	
SM3-002D-4514	P6	58	X	SM3-063D-4506	P7	72	
SM3-002D-4515	P7	47	X	SM3-063D-4507	P7	68	
SM3-002D-4516	P6	60	X	SM3-063D-4508	P6	70	
SM3-002D-4518	P6	52	X	SM3-063D-4509	P6	70	
SM3-002D-4519	P7	53	X	SM3-063D-4510	P6	71	
SM3-002D-4520	P7	47	X	SM3-063D-4511	P8	49	
SM3-002D-4521	P7	59	X	SM3-063D-4512	P7	74	
SM3-002D-4522	P6	60	X	SM3-063D-4513	P7	74	
SM3-002D-4523	P7	57	X	SM3-063D-4514	P7	52	
SM3-002D-4524	P7	59	X	SM3-063D-4515	P7	75	X
SM3-002D-6045	P9	66	X	SM3-063D-4516	P7	75	
SM3-002D-7500	P12	64	X	SM3-063D-4517	P7	76	
SM3-002D-7501	P12	65	X	SM3-063D-7500	P6	67	X
SM3-002D-7503	P12	64	X	SM3-063D-7501	P8	67	X
SM3-002D-7505	P11	63	X	SM3-063D-7505	P8	71	X
SM3-002D-7506	P12	62	X	SM3-064D-4500	P7	76	X
SM3-002D-7507	P12	65	X	SM3-064D-4501	P7	77	X
SM3-002D-7511	P12	63	X	SM3-064D-4502	P7	77	X

Before You Order

Express Delivery
Most orders are processed within 24 hours of receipt. Please allow 7-10 business days for delivery. If you need to place a rush order, please call us by 11:00 a.m. Monday through Friday, 8am-5pm CST and ask for express service (allow 1-2 business days).

Blueprint Price Schedule

Price Code	1-Set	Additional Sets	Reproducible Masters/ PDF Files	CAD
P6	$40	$15	$90	$240
P7	$60	$15	$110	$260
P8	$125	$20	$175	$325
P9	$175	$25	$225	$375
P10	$200	$25	$250	$400
P11	$225	$30	$275	$425
P12	$250	$30	$300	$450
P13	$310	$45	$610	$1000

**Plan prices subject to change without notice.
Please note that plans are not refundable.**

Shipping & Handling Charges

EACH ADDITIONAL SET ADD $2.00 TO SHIPPING CHARGES

U.S. SHIPPING - (AK and HI express only)

Regular *(allow 7-10 business days)*	$5.95
Priority *(allow 3-5 business days)*	$15.00
Express* *(allow 1-2 business days)*	$25.00

CANADA SHIPPING**

Standard *(allow 8-12 business days)*	$15.00
Express* *(allow 3-5 business days)*	$40.00

OVERSEAS SHIPPING/INTERNATIONAL

Call, fax, or e-mail (plans@hdainc.com) for shipping costs.

* For express delivery please call us by 11:00 a.m. Monday-Friday CST

** Orders may be subject to custom's fees and or duties/taxes.

*** An additional set cannot be ordered without the purchase of an initial set or reproducible masters.

NOTE: Shipping and handling does not apply on PDF files. Orders will be emailed within 24 hours (Mon.-Fri., 8-5 CST) of purchase.

Exchange Policies
Since blueprints are printed in response to your order, we cannot honor requests for refunds. However, if for some reason you find that the plan you have purchased does not meet your requirements, you may exchange that plan for another plan in our collection within 90 days of purchase. At the time of the exchange, you will be charged a processing fee of 25% of your original plan package price, plus the difference in price between the plan packages (if applicable) and the cost to ship the new plans to you.

Please note: Reproducible drawings can only be exchanged if the package is unopened and a 25% restocking fee will be charged.

Building Codes & Requirements
At the time the construction drawings were prepared, every effort was made to ensure that these plans and specifications met nationally recognized codes. Our plans conform to most national building codes. Because building codes vary from area to area, some drawing modifications and/or the assistance of a professional designer or architect may be necessary to comply with your local codes or to accommodate specific building site conditions. We advise you to consult with your local building official for information regarding codes governing your area.

The One-Set Study Package
We offer a One-set plan package so you can study your plan in detail. This one set is considered a study set and is marked "not for construction." It is a copyright violation to reproduce blueprints.

Reproducible Masters
If you wish to make some minor design changes, you'll want to order reproducible masters. These drawings contain the same information as the blueprints but are printed on reproducible paper and clearly indicates your right to alter, copy or reproduce. This will allow your builder or a local design professional to make the necessary drawing changes without the major expense of redrawing the plans. This package also allows you to print copies of the modified plans as needed. The right of building only one structure from these plans is licensed exclusively to the buyer. You may not use this design to build a second or multiple dwelling(s) without purchasing another blueprint. Each violation of the Copyright Law is punishable in a fine.

PDF File Format
A complete set of construction drawings in an electronic format that allows you to modify and reproduce the plans to fit your needs. Since these are electronic files, we can send them to you within 24 hours (Mon-Fri, 8-5 CST) via email and save you shipping costs. They also offer printing flexibility by allowing you to print the size and number of sets you need.

Note: These are not CAD files and cannot be altered electronically.

CAD Packages
Many of our plans are available in CAD. For availability, please call our Customer Service Number at 1-800-373-2646.

How To Order

For fastest service, Call Toll-Free
1-800-373-2646 day or night

FOUR Easy Ways To Order

1. CALL toll-free 1-800-373-2646 for credit card orders. MasterCard, Visa, Discover and American Express are accepted.
2. FAX your order to 1-314-770-2226.
3. MAIL the Order Form to: **HDA, Inc.**
   944 Anglum Road
   St. Louis, MO 63042
   Attn: Customer Service Dept.
4. ONLINE visit www.projectplans.com

QUESTIONS?
Call Our Customer Service Number
314-770-2228

Order Form

Please send me -

PLAN NUMBER SM3- _____

PRICE CODE _____ (see Plan Page)

1-Set Plan Package	$ _____
Reproducible Masters (see page 78)	$ _____
CAD Package (call for availability)	$ _____
PDF File (see page 78) (call for availability)	$ _____
One-Set of Plans	$ _____

Additional Plan Sets***

_____ (Qty) at $ _____ each $ _____

SUBTOTAL $ _____

SALES TAX (MO residents add 7%) $ _____

☐ Shipping / Handling (see page 78) $ _____

(each additional set add $2.00 to shipping charges)

TOTAL ENCLOSED (US funds only) $ _____

*** An additional set cannot be ordered without the purchase of an initial set or reproducible masters.

Note: Shipping and handling does not apply for PDF files. Orders will be emailed within 24 hours (Mon.-Fri., 8am-5pm CST) of purchase.

Thank you for your order!

☐ Enclosed is my check or money order payable to HDA, Inc. (Sorry, no COD's)

I hereby authorize HDA, Inc. to charge this purchase to my credit card account (check one):

☐ MasterCard   ☐ VISA   ☐ DISCOVER   ☐ American Express Cards

Credit Card number_____

Expiration date_____

Signature_____

Name_____
(Please print or type)

Street Address_____
(Please **do not** use PO Box)

_____

City _____

State _____ Zip _____

Daytime phone number (_____) - _____

E-mail _____